"FANTASTIC BOOK! F a story. You've got to read this! survived!" – Dellani Oakes, Author and Red River Radio Host

"ONE LIVELY READ! Rico turns the tragedy into a golden account of a ghostwriting assignment gone bad. While his buddy John Dennis Smith honored him with the task of relating how he was the illegitimate, legitimate son of Elvis Presley, the project got swindled from their control. So Rico relates the entire dilemma from the offer to the offing, in a book that rocks with crazy wit, lively banter, and a unique and original cast of cohorts." – Bonnie Lee, Journalist, Ghostwriter, Editor, Reviewer of 'The Virtual Scribe' and Blogger of 'Pour Me Some Grapes'

This is the true story about the legitimate, illegitimate Son of the KING of Rock 'n' Roll, strewn together with the adventures and perils encountered while telling of John Dennis Smith's birthright. His secret has been closeted in the attics of the forbidden for over five decades. Now join me as I take you up the narrow stairway, through the cobwebbed doorway and together we will slowly open the creaking door, creep delicately to the darkened corner, open the dusty, wooden box, pick up the book carefully (we don't want to awaken a sleeping scorpion), open the first page and begin to read the mystery that lies within. – Rico Austin, writer

"I am only at a "July 3rd" entry, but intrigued as to where Rico Austin is taking me." – Amy Perry, Freelance Writer of Downtown Auroran Magazine and Member of Fox Valley Writers

"Rico hits another home run with this Elvis story, his storytelling goes where no writer has gone before! He is a Master of converting a simple description into words of art" – Steve Boyce, Actor and Stuntman

www.RicoAustin.com

In the Shadow of ELVIS

Perils of a Ghostwriter

Rico Austin

A True Story about the Son of the KING of Rock 'n' Roll with the adventures & perils encountered while telling of his secret and birthright.

© 2013, Rico Austin

All rights reserved.
Nuevo Books
Los Ranchos, New Mexico
www.NuevoBooks.com

Printed in the U.S.A.
Book design by Paul Rhetts

No part of this book may be reproduced or transmitted in any form, or by any means, electronic or mechanical, including photocopying, recording, or by any information retrieval system, without the permission of the publisher.

ISBN 978-1-936745-09-8 (pbk. : alk. paper)

Photograph of desert scene: AbleStock / Getty Images
Cover Design and Artwork: Connie Austin
Pictures from the personal collection of John Dennis Smith and Rico Austin

In the Shadow of ELVIS

Perils of a Ghostwriter

Rico Austin

Nuevo Books

Preface

  This is the true story about the legitimate, illegitimate Son of the KING of Rock 'n' Roll, strewn together with the adventures & perils encountered while telling of John Dennis Smith's birthright. His secret has been closeted in the attics of the forbidden for over five decades, now join me as I take you up the narrow stairway, through the cobwebbed doorway and together we will slowly open the creaking door and view the mystery that lies within.

  Dedicated to ALL that have gone on before us, for those that are still with us and to those that shall pass in the future from this world by the cruel hand of cancer of all forms, including HIV and/or AIDS. This story explores a mixture of friendship, forgiveness, love, fear, hate and understanding with a dose of gratitude for life.

  Let us always be thankful for our friends, for our family and for this day. your Amigo, Rico

In the Shadow of ELVIS, Perils of a Ghostwriter

written by Rico Austin

"Maybe tomorrow will be better!"

My mother asked me a few years back if I remember telling her this when I was age eleven or twelve, "Maybe tomorrow will be better." She had been crying at the time, at wits end as her husband, my dad had left us again. She had been alone about six weeks with five young boys at home, I the eldest. I went to my mother, tried to comfort her, putting my arm around her and made this bold statement, "Don't cry Momma, maybe tomorrow will be better."

Many times I've been told, "when You're given lemons, You do make lemonade." After reading this true story, you make the determination of whether you agree.

I have 8 simple sentences of which I live by that cover most of my philosophy for and of life; Each written by a different author during a different time; All profound.

"Do unto others as you would have others do unto you."
[Matthew 7:12] – Bible

"The harder I work, the luckier I get." – Henry Ford

"In order to write about life, first you must live it!"
    – Ernest Hemingway

"Never, never, never give up." – Winston Churchill

"All that is necessary for the triumph of evil is for good men to do nothing." – Edmund Burke

"Every rose has its thorn," – Poison with Bret Michaels

"You'll see the true reflection of me when the tequila bottle is empty!"
    – Rico Austin

"Screw me once, shame on you; screw me twice, shame on me;"
    – (screwed) Author unknown

If the next to the last one on the list, "You'll see the true reflection of me when the tequila bottle is empty," puzzles you, then please, think on this for a moment. Going out drinking with someone for a crazy, late, intoxicated night will give you more in depth insight and knowledge of that person's political views, religious beliefs and personal character than having fifteen lunches with that same human being. If a person does not drink, good luck having a bunch of lunch trying to figure out who he or she really is.

My Precious Readers: warning, keep up if you will and can as this story takes many turns, twists and will take you behind the scenes of ghostwriting, of the unseen literary world's dirty side, of exotic traveled isles and there is a story of the son of Elvis that has never before been shared on paper. It seems that most of us have an Elvis story. One way or another Elvis Presley touched almost all our lives whether it be of a story from our parents, listening to his music or watching one of the many films he brought to life portraying different characters, which each had three things in common – his character was able to play guitar, sing and fall in love with a beautiful girl. I will share my Elvis story and a few others as well; but, none will compare to being the son of the King of Rock 'n' Roll. This 100% true non-fiction novel is of 2 separate books with a few stories that rapidly and slowly intertwine to become one. This experience has definitively changed the way I look at writing another individual's story (ghostwriting), how I view certain literary agents and I am more aware than ever of the many lunatics lurking in the shadows; they do try to destroy our productive lives, our bright futures and our enduring spirits. I do however, believe that these cowards, crazy folk, ass wipes, or whatever we want to call them, can take these afore mentioned precious items from us only if we allow.

On a positive note of writing; I was able to relive some of my past memories through words written and shared. There is a self help, hidden mystery written within the story that I do hope all may see and appreciate. I do enjoy writing and can weave a tale that will have you wanting more. If you dare, if you care, to seek the wonders of the world, it is out there for each of us to touch; for each of us to hold~!

Before we get completely comfy in our easy chair, on the soft leather couch or snuggled into our bed, with the reading light tilted in perfect manner, there is one thing, well a couple of few things that I need to get off my chest, my mind: "Is schizophrenia something that a normal person would try to hide or deny even in the most evident of circumstances?" Or, "if I were truly paranoid, would I try to change the subject from what I originally was writing or saying, to something completely different to cover the depth of what I really knew to be true even though many would think it false?" Is my following statement and quote true?

"The day an individual enters into this world of life is the exact same day that same individual begins their journey towards death!"

Chapter 1
Mortality

Time is of the essence!

October 24th, 2012;

I wonder, "Why I quit gambling, why I gave up Blackjack, the game of 21 that consumed most of my time and my thoughts." I pondered this heavily as I left the office of my personal doctor, Dr. Robert Rauscher Jr. MD late that October morning.

It was one week before Halloween; United Nations Day and I could not have been in a worse nightmare had Count Dracula personally sunk his fangs into my sun drenched neck.

3 months & 21 days earlier is when this story truly begins, perhaps it was even earlier than that.

Chapter 2
Arkansas to Arizona and Beyond

July 3rd , 2012;
Elvis Presley's legitimate, illegitimate son turns 51 years of age today. (This was 10 days before I knew such a man existed).

July 3rd, 2012; 3:05 pm
"Girls just want to have fun," with Cyndi Lauper is blasting through the speakers of my rental car, it's something small, compact. I don't recall the make, model, license plate number or which side the gas tank was on. What I do remember is it smelled of cigarette smoke and I saw residue of ash when I first plopped my tired ass into the seat some odd days ago. Why, did I have to sign the rental agreement, stating, "I would not smoke in 'the little Chevy or Hyundai or whatever it was' or that Avis may apply a cleaning fee of up to $250 for violations to this policy – Details can be found on your Avis rental contract," when clearly some other traveler (and I use the word traveler very loosely) did not crush his or her cigarette to the pavement before getting into the car? Just a question, nothing more; my wife smokes; but she does resist puffing in the car as she respects the resale value should we decide to trade in our 2008 Nissan Xtrerra.

I look at my watch, the watch my Aunt Nettie gave me from Uncle Tom which has the turquoise band he had purchased when visiting Connie and I in Arizona a couple of years back. Uncle Tom had passed away last December 4th in Seattle, Washington while on a visit to see my cousin John and his family. John had been asked what he wanted for his birthday and he had declared to his father, "I want you to come visit me. That is what I would like as my present." My uncle and aunt had flown to Seattle from Boise a few days prior and on John's day of birth plus 46 years to grant John his wish. Uncle Tom passed away that morning in a peaceful way.

My Uncle Tom and Dad had a special connection that spanned less than half a lifetime since Dad passed away in the early 1980s as a young man; both married sisters, but, here comes the kicker. While serving in the U.S. Navy, Uncle Tom had met my Dad's cousin from Arkansas, Jimmie A. Upon completion of their service he had asked Uncle Tom if he would like to join him in his trek down south. Uncle Tom was born and raised in Philadelphia and had never traveled or visited the south, so why not!

After docking in San Diego, California, the twosome hit the road with their savings of nearly four years, hitch hiking to their destination near Pyatt, Arkansas which happened to be by way of Wickenburg, Arizona. My Uncle had told me the story of the first time he had laid eyes on a cactus and how stunning and statuesque they were and of the ride they had caught outside of Phoenix in a red convertible driven by a half drunk man (half sober) headed to Vegas. The man had dropped them off at the Interstate 40 junction and then another vehicle had eventually slowed and stopped. They arrived in the afternoon a couple of days later only to find three trucks and two automobiles stuffed to capacity with everything the family owned. It had resembled the packing of "The Beverly Hillbillies," when Jed, Granny, Jethro and Elly Mae had set off for California. A grand fiesta of possum, grits and chocolate gravy was had that night in the welcoming before the journey to Idaho, land of fruit orchards and vegetable farming galore. Had the son and his buddy been one day later who knows if the neighbors would have given the right state destination, as Iowa is often mistaken for Idaho.

Settlement was agreed upon in the Payette, Idaho area as peaches, pears, cherries and apples were aplenty on the tree. It is here that my Dad and his family had arrived a few years earlier via of Yakima, Washington and had sent word down Arkansas way that the pickins' were aplenty and Idaho was here to stay.

Upon arrival of Uncle Tom with Jimmie and his two brothers Doan and Joe, a couple of their sisters and their parents, another big fiesta was celebrated and that is when my dad-to-be, Tommie met Tom, my uncle-to-be.

Tommie Austin was a handsome, outgoing teenager of eighteen years of age, had ended his schooling at the end of his eighth grade year. He hadn't resisted having had to end his education four years before most of his class. His Father, my grandfather John Wesley Austin had told Dad that he needed to work, to help the family fulltime; no more after school, weekends and summers.

"You need to provide for your family; no ifs, ands or buts," coaxed my granddad.

It didn't matter that Tommie had nearly matched the state high school record for pole vaulting at the age of fifteen and was an upcoming star at center field. It didn't matter that Tommie might have had a sweetheart waiting to walk her to second period class. It didn't matter. That was the way it was during the fifties. And, probably before that.

The Austin family had moved from Yakima, Washington to Fruitland, Idaho as the peaches were rounder and more plump near the Snake River. Tommie was pruning trees, picking fruit and loading bushels of everything on trailers when the eldest son of the rancher asked him, "Wanna work in the cannery?" "It's cooler in there and lots of young dames."

"Yes Sir, thank you Sir!"

It was in the cannery that I became more than hope. My Dad-to-be had met my Mother-to-be, a fiery, redhead from Oklahoma with a temper to match. Tommie and Nina both told matching tales of how they met: "Dad had a tiny squirt gun filled with water and playfully pointed the barrel at my mother while pulling the trigger. Yes, that is how they became acquainted which eventually led to dating, which eventually led to me, which eventually led to five of us little rascals.

Well, during the dating process, my Dad learns of some valuable information, that Nina has a younger sister named Nettie. Tommie and Nina set up Tommie's first cousin's best Navy friend, Mr. Tom H. with Miss Nettie S. and again, five children later history progressed and was added unto.

Why am I describing my family and of where they came and then arrived. Because I know of it and it can be recorded. I have known all the little, insignificant moments from where I entered into this world; but, I have an amigo of whom some of this story is about, that did not find out until he was twenty seven years of age of who his parents were and of his true lineage and heritage.

I am able as is about 99% of our population to reminisce about our beginnings, about our heritage, about our family and from where we and they came from. However, have you considered what the other 1% must be thinking? I am not sure if it is actually is 1% or higher or lower as there is no statistical information on what that actual number is. According to Wikipedia, "The 2000 census was the first census in which adoption statistics were collected. In 2000 the estimated number of adopted children was slightly over 128,000. In 2008 that number increased to nearly 136,000 children." The story that I will write, and you will read of was of an adoption that occurred in 1962.

Part of this memoir novel is the story of a young man that was adopted, raised by a loving family and then later in life found out that his biological father was a person of great significance and interest to the world.

There are a great deal of misconceptions about adoption that worries both the birth parents and the prospective, adoptive families. Birth parents trouble themselves that their adopted child will have ill feelings toward them and adoptive parents may wonder if they will be able to provide love to an adopted child as much as a biological child. This story will provide one child's answer if this is indeed a misconception or if it be truth.

July 3rd, 2012; 5:25 pm

I rubbed my eyes, glanced at my precious watch and wondered where the time had gone. It seemed that I had just left Twin Falls, Idaho after giving a tire repair seminar to one of my favorite customers. It seemed to me that all my customers were in the favorite category. Yes, I had the best of the best in the West. All easy going, all spoke kindly before they growled and if they barked, there was reason. A mere one hundred and twenty miles east was my beginning less than two hours ago and here I was entering the arrival area nearly on time for the 5:20 pm arrival of flight 1613 from Phoenix;

"Wow, what immaculate timing," I congratulated myself approvingly. No phone call, no text, no message. I had outpaced and outraced the nonstop Southwest flight from PHX to BOI. No sooner had I returned my right hand to the steering wheel from patting my left shoulder, the Blackberry had shuddered.

"Damn," I hadn't switched modes from "vibrate only" to "LOUD."

"Hi Babe, yes, of course I'm here." "I'll pick you up outside baggage claim."

I listened, then spoke, "No checked luggage, excellente, see you in a couple."

July 3rd, 2012; 6:50 pm

We cross the bridge where a census sign reads, "Marsing, Population 812." Last time I remembered seeing the sign, it read, "Marsing, Population 510," in the early nineteen eighties. That same sign was there in the early and late nineteen seventies with the population remaining at 510. As kids, we use to joke about it all the time, "Wonder when we leave, if they'll subtract us?"

A banner on Main Street placed on the lights above the railroad crossing greets us or perhaps it is bragging, "The Home of Boise State's Shea McClellin #92." Connie playfully nudges me while jabbing me in the heart with her words, "Looks as if Marsing still doesn't recognize Rico the Author and former Boise State football player."

I gave her a quick grin, pulled the four door whatever it is or was off to the side of the RR tracks, asked for her camera and focused in for a picture of the sign that resonates Marsing. BSU linebacker Shea McClellin a defensive end from Chicken Dinner Road (real address, I changed sprinkler pipes next to that then gravel road) across the river was the 19th pick overall in the first round draft in 2012 by the Chicago Bears. I too had played for the Broncos; but, I had been nearly a hundred pounds lighter, not as quick, but perhaps, just as good at scrabble. And now, was I not an accomplished author with an award winning novel that had given honorable mention to my home town? Where I had first learned of Algebraic expressions from Mrs. Judith McKenzie, Mathematics Educator. Where I first read "The Hobbit," advice given me by Ms. Cynthia Gaede, English Teacher. Where I memorized and recited the Future Farmers of America oath to Mr. Tom Cline, Agriculture and Shop Instructor. Where Mr. Doran Parkins, School Superintendent had taught me to try and take things in stride and stay leveled headed as practiced by Jesus; all in Marsing, Idaho!

The digital camera showed three good photos of the banner and one shitty picture of the car.

It was refreshing, yet difficult to believe that after having traveled around the globe, having lived in the United Kingdom, Lithuania, Mexico and six different states in the U.S., here I was, back in good ol' potato country. Yes, I had always, plans of seeing faraway lands when growing up in Marsing and I had lived up to fulfilling many of my childhood dreams. I took in a deep breath of air, taking in the delightful smell of clover and freshly cut alfalfa, these were just a couple of things that I cherish when returning to Idaho.

Memories of growing up are sometimes welcomed in my mind and at other times are shunned and closeted. I like to think of myself as being normal, the norm, just like everyone else; however, I know that each of us has our skeletons, our insecurities which loosen us from being self assured and completely in control. I believe that I have a brain that uses selective memory and I try to forget the sequences in life that have not been favorable or that put my mind in a frame of non-productive mode.

Two of my three living brothers were already at my mother's home, busy getting lawn chairs unfolded, ready for the grand firework display which would be ignited near the bridge on "the island." I wrapped my arms around my mother and kissed her forehead and then I gave my brothers both a huge hug and handshake. It felt good to be back in my hometown of Marsing, especially during the warm summer days.

I thought of my youngest brother, Steven, who died at the age of ten and of the pain our entire family had suffered upon his death. I was sixteen when it happened and nothing else had mattered to me during those long, sad days afterwards. That was long ago and lots of things had changed since then; but, the pleasant, sweet memory of him as a child had not.

July 4th, 2012;
Next morning, off to McCall (Ski Town USA) in Central Idaho to meet up with amigos and amigas Kory, Michelle, Rich and Rhonda. A spacious modern log cabin near the lake greeted us where Kory and Michelle had invited us to spend the Fourth of July with them. I had scheduled a book signing at the famous Yacht Club where the infamous ordeal of the deck took place some twenty seven years or so ago. LEM (the name he went by were the initials of his first, middle and last name) owned the Yacht Club and was also one of my golfing partners whenever I passed through this tourist town, weather permitting. "My Bad Tequila"

had been promoted for the signing. I had asked LEM what his favorite charity was in town, where 20% of the book sale proceeds could be donated. He favored, 'The Shepherds Home Foundation, Inc.' which has provided hope for countless Idaho children and families. After a grand weekend of water skiing, swimming, biking, hiking, dancing and sipping margaritas, Connie had hitched a ride back to Boise and then to the airport with Rich and Rhonda and I headed north to Coeur d'Alene and then over to the Spokane Valley to continue visiting customers and giving proper tire repair classes to help save lives and sell my products.

July 13th, 2012 (FRIDAY, the you know what!)

My travels had taken me back to Vegas and after one night in that glamour of a glitzy town I was more than ready to sleep in my own bed after having been on the road for a straight eighteen day work trip of the Western U.S. minus the 4th of July fun getaway.

As I neared my home late that afternoon and saw the familiar cacti, I longed to have one cocktail at my favorite cowboy bar in Cave Creek and it is here that my and your Elvis story begins. Still not in my own bed.

Top photo: Wedding Day of Nina & Tommie.
Bottom photo: Mom, Dad & Baby Rico in Payette, Idaho.

Uncle Tom & Jimmy A., Navy Buddies.

Joe A., Uncle Tom H., Doan A. & Tommie Austin (Dad).

Rico's - Uncle Tom, Aunt Nettie, Mom & Dad, all celebrating 20 years of marriage - 1979 Anniversary.

Chapter 3
John Dennis Smith

From the first time I visited Cave Creek in 1991 after moving to the Phoenix metropolitan area from Idaho I've been fascinated with this part cowboy town, with its abundance of cacti species, corrals and watering holes; part tourist town, with its share of boutiques, art galleries and numerous eateries and dining choices. This is also a town of charm that draws its local resident crowd to mingle with strangers and vacationers.

This is the reason I do not find it odd that Cave Creek, Arizona is where I first met the legitimate, illegitimate son of Elvis Presley, the King of Rock 'n' Roll. I was sitting quietly on a stool at the back bar of Harold's Corral, advertised as "THE PLACE in Cave Creek, Arizona for good food, great music and a dang' good time."

I had been at Harold's Corral several times before, whether it be to meet friends for a drink, to have a complete meal, for a book signing or to watch a football game on the extra large, big screen or on one of the many televisions strategically placed throughout the bar and restaurant.

On this particular hot July day, I had come in on Friday, the 13th, late afternoon to cool off from the outside heat and to enjoy some chicken wings on the "Happy Hour" menu for only $2.00. I had been driving most of the day as I was headed to my home in North Scottsdale coming from Las Vegas that morning. I had been in Vegas and prior to that in Idaho for book signings over the 4th of July weekend and figured a nice way to wind down the week would be in Cave Creek. Seated next to me was what seemed like a nice couple carrying on a pleasant conversation with some other folks gathered around the bar, everyone enjoying some appetizers and drink specials. Casually listening to the conversation and people watching as I love to do, I got the feeling that each of them were taxpaying residents of Cave Creek or nearby Carefree. I ordered my wings as medium since I had eaten several different items at one time or other here, but never had tried the wings and didn't want to take a chance on getting HOT wings that might be inferno and send my mouth screaming. The medium wings were quite calm and I overheard the couple next to me ordering the "hot" wings and I casually asked the lady seated directly next to me at the horseshoe shaped bar how their hot wings were as I had ordered the mediums. She answered, "Great, would you like to try a couple?"

I responded, "Sure, I'll trade you a couple of my mediums for a couple of hot ones" and the conversation ensued from there.

"Hello, I'm John Smith and this is my wife Lisa, glad to meet you." I introduced myself to both and before I knew it, the three of us were talking like old friends, which is the norm in Cave Creek. When the subject came up as to what line of work I was in; the words tire repair, sales and author were mentioned and John with his cowboy hat made of felt with more than a few black marker signatures scrawled all over it, wearing a western plaid shirt (like the ones that ex- rodeo champion Larry Mahan used to wear), jeans and leather cowboy boots, casually leaned over and said to me, "You may be just the guy I'm looking for; because, do I have a story for you."

I listened intently to his claim of birthright as that of the Son of the famous, of the one and the only Elvis Presley. After hearing some of the facts and then giving John an autographed hardcover copy of the epic, award winning novel "My Bad Tequila" of which he handed casually to his wife Lisa and said, "She's the reader in the house, if she likes it, then perhaps we'll talk further at a later time."

We had a couple of margaritas, exchanged personal contact information and said our farewells. As I was walking out the door, John called out, "Hey Rico, we've got a tequila party to go to at the lake tomorrow, wanna join us?"

I turned and paced back to the bar where John and Lisa were seated and asked, "What lake and what time?"

"Lake Pleasant, be at our house by 10:00 am." It's gonna be a hoot, "Dirty Tequila" is hosting a party for one of our girlfriend's 40th birthday.

"Hey, being a tequila connoisseur as you stated earlier, have you heard of "Dirty Tequila?"

"No, I haven't."

"Well then Rico, you are in for a treat, we know the owners George and Corwin, a couple of cool Mormon dudes that have developed their own tasty tequila with different flavor additives."

"I'm there amigo, give me directions to your home and I'll see you a few minutes before ten," I gave them both a quick hug of which John climbed down off of the bar stool and was not as tall as what I had first imagined him to be while talking, I would size him up to be (fun size). What John lacks in height he makes up with personality because of his sheer magnetism and energy. I high fived John before exiting the building like I imagined Elvis doing so, hundreds of times before.

The next morning was just as hot as the day before and I was ready to cool off in the lake, north of Peoria, west of the Interstate 17, headed north toward Prescott and then onto Flagstaff. I had been to Lake Pleasant probably thirty times before, it was a manmade reservoir surrounded by thousands and thousands of saguaro cacti and a couple herds of wild burros that would meander down to the lake's edge to quench their thirst with the precious water in the middle of the arid desert. By the time we had met up with the other three carloads of females, all amigas of the birthday girl, it was close to half past eleven, getting warmer by the moment.

Upon arrival at the loading dock, there were two speed boats and a pontoon boat with only men aboard, so much for a great ratio of chicas to chicos. Perhaps, now there were even a few more males than females. The men or hunters had loaded up on drink, both alcoholic and non-alcoholic with a case or two of bottled water to help in the hydration process. The women or gatherers had more than an ample supply of nourishment in the way of chicken, hamburgers, potato salads, casseroles, vegetable trays and chips. There was a raised tarp covering something of importance in one corner of the pontoon. "What's under there?" I asked as we headed out to mark our territory in a certain cove on the water.

"It's my sound equipment and some cases of 'Dirty Tequila,'" the friendly boater announced while lifting back the tarp to give me a peek.

"Right on!" I said while giving a thumbs up.

"Hi, I'm Gary, I'm helping out with my equipment for today's party on the water," said the medium height, middle aged, short haired man in shorts and t- shirt. I extended my right hand, gave my name and we shook by way of hands.

It was a fun-filled day with only a short, single visit from the police patrolling the lake. I didn't know if I would ever see or talk to John again as that is the way it is in Arizona as most everyone is from somewhere else and have their own steady group of friends of whom they hang out with.

Exactly two weeks later, I received a text from John, "Bloody Marys @ harolds now come over ur buying" on a Friday am at 10:02; and then a few minutes later another text comes through at 10:15 am, "Where r u i need a writer." And before I can call, yet another at 10:16 am stating, "Right now."

This is what I love most about John, is that when he makes up his mind to do something it is now! No procrastination and straight to the point! I excitedly called John and told him I could meet with him in about 7 hours.

When we met, his words were, "Great work, Lisa has read your novel "My Bad Tequila" and loved it. We have both agreed that you are the one to help me tell the world of 'My Story.'" I shook hands heartily with John, gave him a brotherly hug and said, "I am honored that you and Lisa have asked me to participate in such an epic journey and exciting project that is extremely personal to you." I too, admitted, I am an Elvis fan. John then told me the name of what he believed would be the name of the biography, "Let the Boy Sing: Elvis Was My Daddy," unless of course I might be able to come up with a better title. It was then that John told me why "Let the Boy Sing." After hearing his story, I agreed that it was indeed a magical title that fit the story well.

And so it began, many meetings, a few great music sessions (I, always hoping John feels like playing and singing a few tunes), and hours and hours of going through John's personal keepsakes, letters, cards, birth certificates and gifts from Elvis Presley and the Presley family.

I remember the first time I heard John Dennis Smith play his guitar and sing a glorious tune of which I had only heard Elvis' recorded voice singing "American Trilogy." After hearing John sing, I thought to myself, "He truly is Elvis's son and has the greatest gift Elvis could have given him – "His Voice."

Chapter 4
Writing and Traveling

Over the next few couple of months I wrote sparsely when I could, met with John occasionally, listening to his stories of growing up and tried to imagine myself being he as a child, he as a boy, he as a young man, he as a middle aged man, he as an adopted happy, musically gifted child, he as discovering and meeting his biological mother, and finally, he as learning that his father was Elvis Presley. As a ghost writer I needed to change his words into descriptive sentences, imaginable feelings, something very readable, magical and somewhat tangible. I tried to think like John and to become John. We had a few things in common, both of our Dads were musicians, both loved women, drink and likewise, as did the both of us. We were indeed our daddies' sons.

John and I had very much in common, our Dads both loved music and sang; we both loved music, John wrote songs and sang. I wrote books, articles and songs; but, I did not have a voice worthy to sing. Both of our Dads were good looking men with sideburns. John's Dad was rich, mine had none. John and I both loved tequila, we shared our love for the agave plant of which a stimulant rose and helped us through many a night.

Fulfilling my duties as a Western Regional Sales Manager covering a territory of eleven states was a difficult challenge for John and I, as sometimes we would go days or weeks without communication. I wrote some in the evenings while in my hotel room; on the weekends, my laptop and notes sprawled across the dining table. The next chapter tells of one of the trips that was planned many months before I had met John and it is one of those times of no communication and very little writing. I include it in this story because a visit to this isolated mass of land of being a significant journey, well worth the time writing about, sharing and reading.

Chapter 5
Iceland – Isle of Extremes, "Fire and Ice"

August 8th, 2012;
Departure from Phoenix to Minneapolis onto Reykjavik.

August 9th, 2012;
Arrival into Reykjavik, Iceland.

My Icelandic amigo Olafur, whom now lives in New York was at the Reykjavik airport at 6:00 am to greet a group of us Americans as we exited through customs. Passport still in my hand, I had picked up a bottle of Patron and a bottle of Sierra Tequila (I had never had as a drink this Sierra Tequila with a red sombrero as a cap) as I briskly picked up other adult beverages at the Duty Free store. We were taken to a lovely breakfast buffet which included a healthy dose of cod oil at the Hilton and then whisked by large van to the Hotel Holt, a quaint first class hotel, Situated on a quiet street, within 5 minutes walking distance from the heart of Reykjavik. Hotel Holt is truly an art gallery within a hotel, representing the largest privately owned art collection in the country of Iceland, as all rooms, hallways, lounges and conference facilities are decorated and complemented with original Icelandic art.

We checked into our lovely hotel, grabbed a quick nap and off on a sightseeing adventure in downtown Reykjavik with our Icelandic, native speaking guide, Mr. Olafur. So many historic buildings, churches, statues to visit and take photos of, as well as modern architectural structures including where the Iceland Symphony Orchestra performs and is widely considered to be one of the leading Nordic orchestras. Fun cafes, restaurants and bars were in abundance as we passed through many on this journey. One of the favorites was the Slippbarinn, a classy little joint down by the harbour, just off the entrance of the Icelandair Hótel Reykjavík Marina. Slippbarinn has its own facebook page with a little map of Reykajavik and the harbor area.

Okay, now to leave the city and see the countryside; we were in for a treat. The entire country is of a scenic wonderland as the landscape changed ever so drastically from moon crater, volcanic rock to rolling hills, meadows to geysers, grand rivers to cascading waterfalls, mountains and glaciers again back to volcanoes rising into the heavens. The sheep and horses of Icelandic lore were ever present with their hoofs making their mark in this faraway land. Icelandic horses' beauty are number one in the world as far as my wife & I are concerned. Their long flowing manes, gorgeous full tails and strong, wide backs were similar to steeds and horses we've read about in fairy tales and epic novels.

"Geysir (Icelandic pronunciation) sometimes known as The Great Geysir, is a geyser in southwestern Iceland. It was the first geyser described in a printed source and the first known to modern Europeans. The English word geyser (a spouting hot spring) derives from Geysir. The name Geysir itself is derived from the Icelandic verb geysa, "to gush", the verb from Old Norse." Only one Icelandic word is used in the English language: geyser. A little language and history lesson is a valuable tool when traveling the globe or for discussion with your children at the dinner table. "Did you know that Geysir ………

The incredible cascading beauty of the waterfall Gullfoss which is ranked as Iceland's most beautiful waterfall and believe you me, Iceland has some waterfalls, all nearly equally spectacular in their own right. Some of us hikers took the wet, slippery, steep trail right down near the falls and felt the power and rush of the water on our faces and throughout our bodies.

Along the highway path, we accumulated some geothermal knowledge at the Hellisheidi geothermal power plant. Most of Iceland's homes and offices generate their electricity and heat from power plants similar to this. (Ok, I do not claim to be a scientist or geothermalist).

Alright now, with all these true facts and stories, are you ready for some real fish tails (tales)?

Believe me folks; it is a good thing that I am writing this section instead of my Texarkana amigo, 'fisherman' Robbie, or the whoppers might not ever come to an end. It begins like this: It was a Friday afternoon, unlike many other Friday afternoons; this one was in Iceland and our tour bus had just left the Gullfoss Waterfall with a busload of drenched, silly acting Americans, to a destination at Holsa Lodge, a fishing getaway for only the rich, famous and friends of Olafur. There to greet us were the exact fitting size, waterproof, insulated, neoprene, chest high, green waders and fishing rods of the fly fishing style and the rod and reel as seen in San Carlos, Sonora, Mexico with the famous International Women's Fishing Team, "Fish 'n' Chicks." We were accommodated with three professional fishing guides, Reynir, Hordur and Olafur. Well, wouldn't you know it, (Olafur) who hooks the first salmon, our trusty guide that was supposed to be helping us catch fish. Being the great guide that we hoped he would be, he traded Ms. Kat her net (she was the first on the scene), for the fly fishing rod and did Ms. Kat ever fight and outwit that man-sized salmon until only this "Woman" stood victorious with the 'Catch of the Day.' That evening laughter was abundant, stories were growing and Viking Beer was flowing in the famous Holsa Lodge where the chess legend Bobby Fischer had fished the same waters in 1972 after claiming victory over Russian, Boris Spassky for the World Chess Championship in Reykjavik during the cold war. Bobby returned to Reykjavik in February 2005 and Iceland's parliament voted in March 2005 to give the American chess player and chess author, Mr. Robert James "Bobby" Fischer RIP (March 9, 1943 – January 17, 2008) full citizenship; he died in Reykjavik.

With the grand photo of Bobby fly fishing in the background and after a gourmet meal prepared by Reynir's brother, the Chef Ingi and Ms. Munda, a feast worthy of Parisians, Romans, the New York / Jersey crowd, Arizonans and Oklahomans was devoured. A celebration or Icelandic tradition was to be followed which involved Ms. Kat catching her first Icelandic Salmon. This tradition is not for the faint of stomach as "Kat Woman" bit the fin from the raw, whole salmon that just hours befor had been swimming, making its final journey up river from the sea to spawn when it was abruptly taken from its surroundings of water and was now going to be someone's supper (after being cooked or smoked). Ms. Kat firmly took a bite out of that salmon and then downed a shot of

"Brennivin," the original Icelandic Schnapps. After the rest of the party took our celebration shot of Brennivin it was time to drink some tequila and get the party rockin' Western style. The Patron went down smooth and Reynir liked the bottle as much as he enjoyed the taste so it was officially given to Reynir to hold, to drink and to protect from this day forward. Next on the list of drinks was to try the Sierra Tequila, just the smell brought tears to my eyes and they were not of joy. I am not going to sugar coat this, I love almost all tequilas in one way or another, but this nasty tequila is responsible for the bad name of tequila. I often hear comments from amigas and amigos that they won't drink tequila because they have had a bad experience. If this is the rank juice that they drank or anything similar then they didn't have a bad experience with tequila, he or she had an experience with bad tequila. I couldn't give this bottle away to a passed out American tourist nor a native, drunk Icelander; no one wanted a part of this, so we just screwed the sombrero back nicely upon its bottle and left it for future, unsuspecting fishermen and fisherwomen tourists. I do hope Reynir finds a home for it, perhaps a troll might enjoy the taste of gasoline with a faint hint of agave.

Now, getting back to the accommodations and food at this "fish camp." I was expecting to rough it with giant, open slats letting in the brisk, cold, night air and an outhouse with a wooden, moon shaped door. Not so, this place had class: six separate bedrooms with two cots in each, accompanied with six separate full bathrooms and showers. Delightful gourmet food, pleasing to even the most discriminate palettes. The presentation of elaborate dishes and service were second to none. Many pictures were taken of the entrees and desserts as they were astonishing in color and decoration. The friendly staff serving us were uniquely hospitable and did everything to provide us with complete comfort.

Two others in our group were able to convince a salmon to take their lures, amigos, David W. of Tennessee and Tim S. of Missouri.

Warning: Do not eat shark at fish camp!!! Another story!!!

A real journey is not epic until a near death, defying experience occurs and this was a "Real, Epic Journey." Being stuck in the mud was a terrifying experience as I had my left leg stuck in deep mud to my crotch and the other leg was only a few inches deep into the river on more solid ground. Reynir tried to get me out, but to no avail, then he said those words that crept eerily into my spine, "You're really stuck, I don't know how we are going to get you out." It seemed like the longest ten minutes of my life and the water seemed to be getting deeper (even though it was not) and I was beginning to panic. I rocked my body, back and forth, further centimeter by further centimeter with Reynir and Dana tugging at me until, finally freedom; "Escape from the Iceland River Mud," may be the next best seller.

The trip ended in great fashion as it would have been incomplete without a journey to the world renowned BLUE LAGOON; soothing our achy, fish casting bodies which had indulged in too many tasty meals and alcoholic beverages. There is a rumor that Heidi Klum and Claudia Schiffer were hanging with us at the "Lagoon," fresh off the set of filming together in Iceland. This visit to the Blue Lagoon ended a spectacular adventure in style.

After we were taken to the airport for our departures and we had made our way through security, there was still plenty of time for shopping at the Duty Free store. I spotted a giant size, thick book with the title of, "Learn Icelandic in Two Minutes." Interested and intrigued I picked it up, thinking perhaps I can learn this Nordic language. I opened the box and there was a bottle of "Brennivin," the original Icelandic Schnapps and two shot glasses. I purchased three "books," two of which were for gifts and one for me. When I returned home to Arizona, I opened the bottle, poured myself a double shot, (one shot in each glass) and behold; now I can "Speak like a Viking."

I have been on many trips in my lifetime and this is one that will forever be frontal in my memory. This is not the end; however, this does conclude our story of ICELAND, an Isle of Extremes, "FIRE and ICE."

Iceland Countryside.

Icelandic Horses.

Connie & Rico at Gullfoss Waterfall.

Blue Lagoon with face mud.
Back Row: Rico, Kat, Dana, Connie, Gibbo, Donna
John, Ann, Clint -- Front Row: Tim, Jen

29

Rico fishing in an Iceland River.

Holsa Lodge, Fish Camp.
Back Row: Rico, Reynir, Brian, Olafur, John, Tim, Gibbo, Robbie
Front Row: Dana, David, Kat, Hordur, Connie

Chapter 6
Dystel and Goderich Literary Management

The next few weeks were uneventful, working, writing and writing, working, except for a Labor Day, long weekend trip down south of the border, in San Carlos, Sonora, Mexico. This is the new Cabo, brilliant white sand beaches with cacti reaching out to the Sea of Cortez. There was an eventful night preceded by a swim in the Sea of Cortez and a Dos Equis XX (of the most interesting man in the world fame) at the Soggy Peso aka Hang Out after an afternoon at the marina watching the fisherman come in and weigh their catch during the Cantina Cup Fishing Tournament with several amigos and amigas including Captain "Wild" Bill Wichrowski of "Deadliest Catch" fame, Abby and Kim C., Jim and Jana L., Bryan and Lisa R., Connie, Alexis and myself at Ruby's Wine Bar located on the marina.

During these next weeks, I got to know John better, each session we had. At times, he would take out his guitar and sing with reverence in his voice. John loves to sing gospel songs; I believe he prefers that genre of music to that of country; but, have been afraid to ask as I do not want to disappoint what I believe.

Soon after we had agreed that I would write John's story, this is when I found out that another author was or had been involved. John had asked me to wait until he had completely severed ties with his original collaborator, Karen Albright Lin of whom John had met through Karen's colleague and fellow writer, Suzanne Handler in March of 2012. This news sent a shiver right to the edge of my fingers, where my prints were

31

unique to me. Disturbing does not describe how I felt as I tried to put myself in Ms. Albright Lin's footwear, thinking that I would soon be writing a true story that is unique and interesting in every way, a story that writers dream of having the opportunity to pen. And, then to have it so abruptly taken away.

I told John that, "I did not want to be involved if there was any chance of a lawsuit." John's response was, "Hell, my lawyer told me that Karen has no grounds for a case as we have given her three opportunities to submit a good proposal to her agent Jane Dystel. Besides, a lawsuit wouldn't be all bad, as any publicity would mean more book sales for us."

Now I had many questions for John: "Who is Jane Dystel?" "How much has Karen written already for you?" "What has Karen written in the past?" "Is there a chance this will happen to me?"

All of my questions were answered one by one: Jane Dystel is a literary agent of Karen Albright Lin and she had pitched the story to Jane, founding member and co-owner of Dystel & Goderich Literary Management which was founded in 1994 by Jane Dystel. Jane had been a respected figure in publishing for over 30 years — first as an editor, then as a publisher, and finally as an agent for authors.

Karen had written a proposal of sixty pages which were later shared with me. Three proposals later, Jane Dystel and partner, Miriam Goderich were still not satisfied with any of the proposals. Even after Karen was advised to follow to the exact specifications and format to the book proposal, "The Courage to Hope, How I Stood Up to the Right Wing Media, the Obama Administration, and the Forces of Fear" by Shirley Sherrod with one of the most respected ghostwriters in autobiographies, Catherine Whitney who helped pen Lee Iacocca's biography.

I was astounded upon hearing that Karen had been sent a book proposal of a book that had not even come out on the market yet and that she had refused to follow the format, given her as a successful guide.

September 23rd, 2012;
I receive the following email from John D. Smith with attachment:
From: John D Smith
Sent: Sunday, September 23, 2012; 11:27 am
To: Rico Austin

Subject: Courage to Hope Proposal

I call John to tell him I have received the book proposal. He tells me to follow it as per Jane Dystel and that he needs me to have a proposal completed and ready to send to Jane and Miriam in three weeks. "Oh, and by the way, I don't think Jane is really supposed to send us the proposal, so please don't share this document with anyone."

A dilemma of an author had struck me. "Should I open the document?" Would I want a fellow writer or a literary agent doing this same thing to me?" Absolutely not, but I am of a curious nature and clearly see myself as an opportunist. Yes, I would look at this proposal, study this proposal and submit my proposal based upon this proposal which was sent to me. It made sense to do this, especially if I did indeed want to co-author with John Dennis Smith this project and have it accepted by Dystel and Goderich Literary Management to pitch it to publishers.

My weakness prevailed as the greater strength.

Now I have doubts about this project; I have doubts about the professionalism of one of the most respected and largest literary agents in North America. I still do not have an official contract, just a shake of hands by John that we will split 50 / 50 proceeds of the book after Jane Dystel takes her cut of 15% off the top. But, as John always stated to me whenever I mentioned having a full contract and agreement spelled out, "That is how Elvis did business and how I was taught to do business in the south, with the shake of the hand. This is my bond and my word."

I was given until Monday morning, October 15th, 2012 to complete my first book proposal.

For every single evening, Monday thru Friday and all day on Saturday and Sunday, I pored over every word, every section, every part of Shirley Sherrod and Catherine Whitney's work. All thirteen pages of the "Overview," the seven pages of "The Market for The Courage to Hope," the twelve chapters, including the Sample Chapter which was Chapter One: "The White House Wants You Out." Fifty and five double spaced pages made up this proposal. The entire time, I am wondering, "Have Shirley and Catherine given their consent to have Dystel and Goderich Literary Management emailing their literary work of art around the country?" I am thinking to myself, "As a writer I know that I would not feel comfortable having my work sent through hyperspace even before my novel is available on bookshelves."

October 8th, 2012; 4:48 am

An email comes in from Annette Snyder, the founder, author and blogger of the popular, "Fifty Authors from Fifty States Blog" which features a single, prominent or up and coming author from each of the states to write a 250 – 550 word story about her or his state. Annette has announced to me that I have been selected to represent my Great State of Arizona and that my writing will be published and available for viewing on her website http://annettesnyder.blogspot.com the week of May 19th, 2013.

I'm thrilled to have finally been selected from the list of Arizona finalists and will be able to showcase my two new books of 2013 as well as my previous novel in the same year as our state's 101st Birthday.

October 15th; 3:40 am

"Let the Boy Sing, Elvis was My Daddy" book proposal is finished, all sixty nine written pages. Now to rest.

October 15th; 1:58 pm
From: John D Smith
Sent: Monday, October 15, 2012; 1:58 pm
To: Jane Dystel
Cc: Rico Austin
Subject: Proposal - Let the Boy Sing, Elvis was my Daddy
Hello Jane,

I am here with Rico and he has completed the proposal for "Let the Boy Sing, Elvis was my Daddy." My wife, Lisa & I have proof read it and I believe it to be a great work and I am sure you will be very pleased with it. I have copied Rico as well, so for any future correspondence he can be copied. Thank You & Best Regards, John

October 15th, 2012;
We received the following response from Jane Dystel:

From: Jane Dystel
Subject: RE: Proposal - Let the Boy Sing, Elvis was my Daddy
To: "John D Smith"
Cc: "Rico Austin"
Date: Monday, October 15, 2012; 2:01 pm
Glad to have this John and we will be back to you soon. Jane
Jane Dystel
Dystel & Goderich Literary Management
One Union Square West Suite 904
New York, NY 10003 www.dystel.com
(Ph) 212 --- ----, ext. 12 (Fax) 212 --- ----

Connie & Wild Bill from Deadliest Catch.

Jim L., Wild Bill & Abby C. in San Carlos, Mexico.

Chapter 7
The Proposal

(Special Note) This is the proposal in its entirety that was sent to Dystel & Goderich Literary Management. It has its own chapters all within (this) Chapter 7.

Book Proposal

LET the BOY SING
ELVIS WAS MY DADDY; THE UNTOLD STORY

By John Dennis Smith
with Rico Austin

OVERVIEW

A black 1958 Cadillac pulled up through the gates of the Nursing School in Monroe, Louisiana, briefly stopping at the front entrance door as a dark haired, young lady exited clutching a small handbag and a hand written note. While faintly looking nervous on November 14th, 1960 she slid into the front seat of the classic automobile with car door closing quickly behind her; The car stealthily sped away as one of the student nurses riding her bicycle to one of her classes saw Elvis at the steering wheel as he kissed the fair skinned, auburn haired girl sitting next to him of whom she recognized as possibly, yes, definitely that being of fellow student Zona Marie, who hesitantly gave a slight wave of the hand and a huge smile that only a young girl in love…..

June 1988:
I'm visiting my sister in Ahwatukee, a town that is part of the Phoenix, Arizona metro area when the first bomb shell of my secret, previously unknown part of my life had been dropped on me. My older sister had risen much earlier that morning than I, as she was headed to work and had told me the night before to fend for myself. I lazily opened the silverware drawer and fumbled for a spoon; but when closing the drawer, it didn't close smoothly. I tried to fix it and that is when I saw a yellow, faded corner of an envelope and tugged at it. The name addressed was John Dennis Smith (my name) and I gasped. I knew the name, but had never seen the written spelling of the post marked addressor's name: Zona Marie. Why was there a card with my name on it, but with my sister's address? Why was it hid in her silverware drawer? Was this the same Zona that I had known as a close friend who had visited my sisters and I when a toddler and growing up? Why was I nervous and scared at the same time? All of these questions were filtering through my mind as I frantically tore open the envelope. "Happy Birthday Son," was what I remembered seeing as I read the best wishes.

This is my story; but, for it to be told truthfully and fully, many secrets must be explored of my family, both my adoptive parents and my natural parents. Many of my life's previously closed and locked doors must be opened to give this story justice and untangle many webs of the greatest Elvis mystery told.

ELVIS PRESLEY was my Daddy!!

I was adopted and raised by Gladys Love Presley's (formerly Gladys Love Smith) younger, half brother I.D. Smith and his wife Etta Smith and was raised in a Christian home and by a GOD fearing family. Yes, Gladys Presley – the mother of Elvis Presley. My two older half-sisters and I were adopted by my Great Uncle who was of the same blood of Elvis and of me. He and my Great Aunt by marriage of Elvis had agreed to take us in and to care for us.

My childhood was incredible, full of music and instruments as I was weaned on Gospel and Country Music by my caring and nurturing, aged, adoptive parents. There were 3 nurse maids all of black color as I was raised in Louisiana, this was somewhat common in the early sixties in the south.

On the day of my birth in July 3rd, 1961; a man, my biological father, Mr. Elvis Presley disguised as an older, close friend of the family viewed his premature baby son. With him was one of his dearest and most trusted confidantes, singer – Sherrill 'Shaun' Neilsen. Elvis being the caring, good hearted and loyal person that we all have heard and read stories about came to see Zona Marie and their newborn child on that very same day that he had received word that Zona was in the hospital and expecting to give an early birth to a premature baby. I am the "love child" or as others may say, "the result" of those three days of intense love in November; the 14th, 15th and 16th. Those very same three days are the only time in Elvis's career of which he was not accounted for and his whereabouts unknown to the world. Elvis had been with my mother for three days and nights somewhere at a hotel between Monroe and Shreveport, Louisiana.

I have pieced together most of my life that was hid from me for the better half of most of my years on Earth. The mystery, the secrecy, the adoption was for the protection of several individuals; firstly, that of the good, for the icon of Rock 'n' Roll, Mr. Elvis Presley. It would have been very detrimental for his image to have fathered a child with a separated woman from a marriage that would soon end in divorce. A woman who had two previous children from that marriage. Next, the hush, hush was for the protection of my mother who was a young woman, separated from her husband and a soon-to-be divorcee. She would have come under scorn from family and friends, most likely for the rest of her long life and would be shunned. The secret of my birthright and heritage of my biological parents was also to protect me in my early childhood years from the pressures of being a bastard son, of being a raised without a father. Yes, the secret also protected me from being an outcast, of being ridiculed and alone.

I often now think what my life would have been, how differently it might have turned out, had one thing changed such as Elvis not deciding to continue seeing, pursuing and dating a young teenage girl. I speak of Ms. Priscilla Beaulieu of whom Elvis would eventually marry after a long and drawn out courtship that spanned seven and a half years of whom he had met in Friedberg, Germany while stationed there immediately upon completion of training.

Yes, I often dwell on that fact: of what my life would have been and how different my path might have been had the King of Rock 'n' Roll, my Daddy not listened to his handlers, managers and close confidantes and would have listened to his heart and stayed with my mother Zona Marie instead of ……..

Would I still long for the spotlight and the stage?

How would I have taken my Daddy's death when the news of his passing was heard round the world on that fateful day of August 16th, 1977 as I was barely 16 years of age.

Would I have known for sure, if that indeed was the day that my Daddy had passed on from this world?

This is one of the great puzzles in life that actually makes sense, if only one thing is done differently during our life then everything changes from that moment on; sometimes it could be minor such as deciding not to get in the truck with some drunk friends that could have led to death or dismemberment. Or, deciding to go out on that blind date that could lead to marriage and then later on down the road, I'm hoping for death at least for one of the two of us, not caring in particular which party it is. That last sentence goes out to one of my three ex wives that fortunately has finally chosen to move on.

I've fathered a child (a son) of my own, only to have been told on the phone that he had been killed at age 17 by a drunk driver during the night. I've discovered truths and I've uncovered lies. It is with conviction that I now believe, is the time to tell the world of my story which I had been asked to keep it a secret until the time was right. The "time has come" for the world to read and learn of "Elvis' Untold Story" of his legitimate, illegitimate son; therefore, "LET the BOY SING: ELVIS was my Daddy."

A life on the road and at home

I have had a full lifetime of pleasures, riding the highest wave of what this world had to offer to the other end of the spectrum of disappointments leading to the lowest points of misery and despair where I no longer wanted or cared to pull my boot straps up and take in another day. We all have our stories, our tales of which most are worth the reading or listening. The reason my story is of even greater interest is because of who my Daddy was.

My life has taken on a great many side stories from singing with my adopted father in a small church, to being invited to dance upon stage with relatives on the Lawrence Welk show to being asked by Lawrence Welk himself to join "his" show as the youngest, permanent, performing member. Of traveling for 2 years with the Lawrence Welk troupe at the young and influential age of sixteen. I sang as a backup singer, I sang as lead singer with backup singers. I have sang solo and with some of Country's Greatest Stars of Nashville. I am now currently recording two albums and occasionally strum my guitar and sing for my neighbors and tourists in a couple of country bars in Cave Creek, Arizona, the small southwestern town where I now call home and hang my cowboy hat. Once in a while, someone will shout out, "Johnny Boy, would you please sing "American Trilogy" of which I oblige and the house will come down afterwards with thunderous applause as only I and one other baritone can hit that "High C Note." Yes, you have probably guessed that other person I speak of, is none other than Elvis Presley, my Daddy.

There are a great many coincidences between my famous Daddy and me. Elvis won three Grammy Awards—his only Grammies—and they were for his Christian gospel songs, "How Great Thou Art" (Sacred category, 1967), "He Touched Me" (Inspirational category, 1972), and again "How Great Thou Art" (Inspirational, Non-classical category, 1974) . I've also sung both "How Great Thou Art" and "He Touched Me." Elvis's album, "He Touched Me," was featured on a documentary on PBS. Uncanny is the fact that I also recorded a gospel album, "He Touched Me," with the same songs in the same order as my daddy—without knowing about the coincidental fact. After we finished recording, it was pointed out to me by

Michael McClain, my engineer and producer.

Elvis Presley, I.D. Smith and I all three sang at different times on the "Louisiana Hayride."

My father, my mother and I have all had our share of lovers, heart break and other disappointments when it came to romance and love. I have been married four times, and my mother has been married six different times and Elvis though having been married only once had more than his share of lovers and girlfriends.

My time on the road as a lead singer with very well known bands and bands of obscurity, little known except for the locals in that vicinity of where we performed or began. I have been fortunate to have been associated and singing lead with "Tejas," "Restless Heart," "Southern Thunder," "The John Dennis Smith Band," "Borrowed Money" and "Wolf Creek."

H.T. (Harrison Tyner) was my hand selected manager by Elvis. H.T. was a close friend and confidante of Elvis, H.T. was a close friend of Sherrill "Shaun" Nielson and most importantly, H.T. is my friend to this day. I received a hand written letter from Harrison Tyner, my lifelong manager on August 5, 1991.

> J.D.,
> As I discussed with Sherrill and your mother, it is not the time to expose your father. And we made a promise we will keep you safe. When the time is right, we will stand behind you then as we do now. HT

Being a first born, only son and descendant of Elvis, I have many keepsakes and valuable mementos including personal photos of Elvis, my Mother, Priscilla, Lisa Marie, Glen Campbell and of me which have never before been published nor have been seen by the public. A few of these photos are of only Elvis and I. These are photos of Father and Son. I have the DNA results showing that Elvis Presley is 99.9% confirmed as fathering John Dennis Smith. My birth mother, Zona Marie went to Hidalgo County, Texas in 2009 to retrieve my original birth certificate and placed in my hands the officially sealed Birth Certificate showing her as my Mother and Elvis Aaron Presley as my Father.

After I was told the truth, I discovered that many friends around

Elvis and me knew of my heritage and birthright. They'd kept it from me as a favor to Elvis.

As I continue to tell my story, you will begin to see that for the most part I do not have regrets and have had a great life of 51 years thus far. When I think about Elvis and his ending of life at forty two years, if indeed he passed on in 1977. Or? Did he possibly live to be forty nine years, if my Daddy did die in 1984 as I truly believe he did as I have evidence (E.P.'s folded military flag was sent to me from the Rose-Neath funeral home in Louisiana in 1984. It has always been a mystery as to why there was no flag draped on his casket in 1977 even though Elvis had served in the Armed Forces) of why I feel so strongly about this. I have My Father's Military Flag. My Daddy, Elvis Presley, the King of Rock 'n' Roll died a young man and well before he should have left this world. A world that loved him and adored his music. I would have loved to have known this man, this legend as a friend and as a caring, nurturing Father to me.

This is a story of my birthright, of my triumphs and of my trials, of being put out into the world by my own mother for adoption and her heartache, later regrets and sad memories at making that long since done decision.

This is an untold, closeted story of a world renown, young Elvis and of a unknown, young woman named Zona Marie deeply in love with a man that she could not marry and could not share with the world of her love for this man.

The Market for Let the Boy Sing: Elvis was my Daddy

Ever since finding out that Elvis Aaron Presley was my Father over 2 decades ago, on my 27th birthday I have known that I would write and share with Elvis' fans of this widely unknown adventure and mystery of the King of Rock 'n' Roll, sometime during my life.

This story shall be told from the heart and with honesty; it will include all the love, hate, truth and passion that make up living carefree while young, growing into adulthood and eventually realizing my own mortality. The country and the world around are all interested in personal true stories of conflict, of secrets, of passion, of love. It will also give an in-depth look at Nashville and some of its greatest members and players.

The interest is multiplied and much greater when a celebrity or famous person is whom the novel is written about and when it is verifiably a true story spoken and told from the heart.

Let the Boy Sing: Elvis was my Daddy is timed to take advantage of the ever growing need of collections for more Elvis Presley items and stories. The readership will be diverse over many age segments and demographics as Elvis followers have been and are of every age, color, national origin, sex, and religion. However, this being said, the largest market will be female baby boomers (born 1946 – 1964) and both female and male gender that were born between 1930 – 1945 which combined will cover one of the single largest demographics ever imagined possible for this type of book release. This is a marketer's dream come true and we will be right in the middle of it as this autobiography makes history.

Elvis has sold more recordings than anyone in history according to the Guinness Book of World Records. A recent Elvis compilation album, Elvis 30 #1 Hits, went straight to the charts, hitting number one in the UK. According to a 2005 Harris Interactive poll, nearly one-third of all Americans have bought Elvis records, videos or CDs.

50,000,000 Elvis Fans Can't Be Wrong: Elvis' Gold Records - Volume 2 is the ninth album by Elvis Presley, issued on RCA Victor Records in November 1959. It is a compilation of hit singles released in 1958 and 1959 by Presley, from two recording sessions in June 1958 at RCA Studios in Nashville and three at Radio Recorders in Hollywood. The album peaked at #31 on the Billboard Top Pop Albums chart, and is considered to be one of the most successful and influential compilation albums of all time. It was certified Gold on 11/1/1966 and Platinum on 3/27/1992 by the R.I.A.A.

There are more than 500,000,000 Elvis fans worldwide. Out of them, 90% purchase anything related to Elvis, most items costing $10.00 and up. Official Elvis fan club members and countless others spend hundreds of millions of dollars each year on all things Elvis. Records, books, playing cards, watches, stamps, and a plethora of other paraphernalia bring premiums on e-bay and elsewhere.

Elvis fans eagerly await all books about their idol. Even those books or autobiographies written by Elvis wannabes and others claiming to be the offspring of the King of Rock 'n' Roll, including Swedish Lisa Johansen who claimed to be the real, whisked-away Lisa Marie Presley in her 1998 memoir I, Lisa Marie: The True Story of Elvis Presley's Real Daughter (self published,1998). Her tabloid tale earned her an undisclosed amount. Return to Sender: The Secret Son of Elvis Presley by Les and Sue Fox (West Highland Publishing Company, 1996) is light fiction speculating that Elvis may have cloned himself to have a son.

One of the best selling Elvis books of all time was Is Elvis Still Alive? (Tudor, 1988) In it, Gail Brewer-Giorgio excites the curiosity of the public about the speculations that Elvis did not die when and how the public was told. It sold more than 1,000,000 copies. (http://www.elvisnews.com/news.aspx/best-selling-elvis-books/5716)

Many other books about the cultural icon continue to fascinate the public: all- time best selling Elvis book, Priscilla Presley's story written with Sandra Harmon, Elvis and Me (Berkley, 1986) and the sex involving orgies tell-all biography by Country music journalist, Alanna Nash— Baby Let's Play House: Elvis Presley and the Women Who Loved Him (HarperCollins, 2010). Special note: There's no mention of Zona Marie in any previous books. Her love affair with Elvis was a secret, well kept by the close friends that knew of the tryst and of the son that was begat from that secret love meeting.

It is no surprise that other revealing and suggestive books do remarkably well, especially when previously undiscovered love affairs are involved. Familiar examples include Full Service: My Adventures in Hollywood and the Secret Sex Lives of the Stars by Scotty Bowers and Lionel Friedberg (Grove Press, 2012) and Tell-All, a celebrity kiss-and-tell book by Chuck Palahnink (Anchor, 2011). Mine is a tell all, of royal magnitude.

There is an entire classification of books devoted (but not limited to) visitors of Graceland including: Graceland: The Living Legacy of Elvis Presley by Chet Flippo (Collins Pub San Francisco,1993) and Graceland: An Interactive Pop-Up Tour by Chuck Murphy, Jason Rekulak, Kevin Kosbab and Priscilla Presley (Quirk Books, 2006).

There are countless and more importantly, successful Elvis biographies such as two books by Peter Gurlnick, Last Train to Memphis : The Rise of Elvis Presley (which sold over 1,000,000 copies) and *Careless Love: The Unmaking of Elvis Presley (*Back Bay Books, 2000). The fascination carries over to his wife in books like Child Bride: The Untold Story of Priscilla Beaulieu Presley, a biography by Suzanne Finstad (Three Rivers Press, 2006).

Books about children of celebrities having lasting power and superb popularity. How's Your Dad?: Living in the Shadow of a Rock Star Parent by Zöe Street Howe (Omnibus Press, 2010) explores the life of children of iconic rock 'n' roll figures, like Julian Lennon following in the footsteps of his famous Beatle father, Mr. John Lennon. There are other books about children stepping out of the shadows of their famous parents such as In His Footsteps: Famous Fathers & Celebrity Children by Birqit Krols (Tectum Publishers, 2011).

Voyeuristic readers purchase books that expose celebrities' love children. Eddie Murphy: The Life and Times of a Comic on the Edge by Frank Sanello depicts the complex life and intimate demons of the comic actor (Birch Lane Press, 1997). One of the greatest political downfalls of any politician happened to John Edwards as adultery led to a pregnancy and then an unacknowledged lovechild. His story was told by Andrew Young in The Politician: An Insider's Account of John Edwards's Pursuit of the Presidency and the Scandal That Brought Him Down (Thomas Dunne Books, 2010).

Also, gaining large readership are collections of interviews and mini biographies of children of celebrities, some emphasize the overwhelming depression and unhappiness, exemplified by On the Edge of the Spotlight: Celebrities' Children Speak Out About Their Lives by Kathy Cronkite (Warner Books, 1982) and Malcolm Forbes and Jeff Bloch's What

Happened to Their Kids: Children of the Rich and Famous (Simon & Schuster, 1990).

Contrary to typical expectations and beliefs, my experience growing up as a musical prodigy in the public eye was a good one. There are a great many child stars that have had tremendous difficulties being raised in public. Often they get caught up in substance or alcohol abuse, while some even become suicidal. Michael Jackson would be a good example of an unhappy prodigy, as one can read in his autobiography, Moonwalk (Crown Archetype, 2009). Young actors, too, suffer such fate, such as Corey Feldman of The Goonies—The Corey Feldman Handbook: Everything You Need to Know About Corey Feldman by Emily Smith (Tebbo, 2012) and Gary Coleman of Different Strokes—Gary Coleman: Medical Miracle by the Coleman family and Bill Davidson (Putnam Publishing Group, 1981) . But unlike Patty Duke's wildly popular nightmare, child actor story Call Me Anna: The Autobiography of Patty Duke (Bantam, 1988), my true story is not focused on the trials of having a creative gift so much as I recall and write of triumphs, the people and the interesting places that my voice allowed me to visit.

Since these revelatory books about the offspring of celebrities can succeed, imagine the sales potential for one that explores what it's like to be born the child of a celebrity, living in an adopted household, have the truth hidden from him, and then to have his own taste of fame. And then finally, to discover that his biological father was the most famous Rock 'n' Roll singer in history.

Let the Boy Sing: Elvis was my Daddy will have another very interesting element of my life - Adoption. My experience didn't leave me with self doubt and resentment; but, obviously it did affect me. There are quite a few reference books about loss, grief and other unique issues some adoptees have faced. Twenty Things Adopted Kids Wish Their Adoptive Parents Knew by Sherrie Eldridge (Delta, 1999) addresses these difficult experiences. When a child asks for details, the truth may be painful, even traumatic. Telling the Truth to Your Adopted or Foster Child: Making Sense of the Past by Betsy Keefer and Jayne Schooler (Praeger, 2000) takes this angle. My story is unique in that I faced unusual challenges, such as having my musical and personal life orchestrated at times only to discover whose famous hand may well have been behind most of it.

A quick search of the Internet suggests that Elvis being my father will draw a huge number of readers to my memoir. An Amazon.com Elvis book search nets over 7,200 returns. A Google search, "Article Elvis 2012," turns up over 51,000,000 results.

Elvis is gone, but not forgotten. An estimated 20,000 fans held a candlelight vigil 34 years after Elvis's 1977 death.

He's remembered through other technology that didn't exist while he was alive. An on-line search for blogs about Elvis Presley nets over 12,000,000 results, many of the blogs are quite active, including historical blogs such as the "Elvis Presley History Blog" which profiles the King and educates the reader on his life and legacy (http://www.elvis-history-blog.com).

Elvis Presley's popularity is not going away. According to a Harris Interactive poll, more than 176 million Americans have had their lives touched by Elvis in some way or form; 71 million plus Americans consider themselves Elvis fans. Of these fans 60 percent are female and 70 percent are ages 26 -55; 75% have claimed to have purchased collectibles.

Music lover demographics bode well for my book. A search engine will net tens of millions of results for gospel blogs. My focus has been on both gospel and country music. Elvis set family precedence for this genre. His three Grammy Awards, his only Grammies, were for his Christian gospel songs.

There are more than 1,400 radio stations that play nothing but gospel music, representing 80 million listeners. It is one of the fastest-growing genres in the industry. (http://www.gospel860.com/index.php?option=com_content&view=article&id=65&Itemid=71)

Searching the Internet draws hundreds of millions of results for country music blogs. There's an enormous market for country and western music as 38% of American Adults are country music fans, making up 85 million people. 64% of those are between the ages of 25-54, prime consumers with disposable income.

Not only is the market of Elvis in the United States, there is approximately 20% in the foreign market and they are very easy to reach and to sell today. Three decades after the year the world believed he died,

Elvis is the most impersonated rock 'n' roll celebrity. A gathering of these look-alikes are not only in Las Vegas; some are entertaining tourists at resorts in India. In Amsterdam an entire record store is devoted to Elvis recordings. The U.K. still drives Elvis albums to the top of the charts. EP Enterprises, Inc. estimates that, over time, 40% of all Elvis's record sales have been outside the U.S., more than 400 Million Records. (http://www.elvis.com/about-the-king/achievements.aspx)

Elvis Presley Enterprises alone serves up more than 400 official fan clubs and others continue to pop up. EPE has online members joining every day, paying up to $40 to receive updates on Elvis events, merchandise and news. This book will be BIG NEWS.

Marketing is something I do extremely well. It's no small task for most musicians to keep themselves busy with gigs. I have contacts in the world of music and among church groups that keep me entertaining from week to week, be it local or on the road.

I thrive in public venues and I'm now eager to address the press. Most authors dream longingly of making TV appearances. I've already experienced it. I was on several noon talk shows in Nashville and was on 'Pop Goes the Country' with Ralph Emery. I believe my revelation makes this marketing opportunity a sure thing. Stations will likely fight for my time, and viewers won't be disappointed. I can own an audience. As future readers will be charmed by what my friends call my "inherited charisma," they'll be drawn in by my story and learn things about the King that many people don't know. Some may be surprised to tune into a primetime interview on CNN and see that Elvis's son has auburn hair, a fact made less puzzling when they learn that Elvis was naturally auburn, meticulously honed his physical appearance, and chose to dye his hair.

In addition, Internet chatter creates many opportunities for me to advertise and promote the release of Let the Boy Sing: Elvis was my Daddy.

Social media and the tabloids will have a hay day when word gets out, sparking yet another firestorm of exposure and huge sales. This will be much larger than recent stories exposing the love children of John Edwards, Jessie Jackson, and Arnold Schwarzenegger.

I will go beyond standard social media promotion and talk show appearances. My lifestyle is music and music is my advertising. I'll combine book signings with concerts. And each new album I record will only add to the appeal of this revelatory book. Friends, as well as Rico, will be happy to team up with me for marketing activities and use social media to promote Let the Boy Sing: Elvis was my Daddy, for example: creating an "I love Elvis's Son" Pinterest board.

Let the Boy Sing: Elvis Was my Daddy will reintroduce me and my music to the world and have readers worldwide discovering a new "chapter" in Elvis' secret life and will have DJs spinning the albums of Elvis and John Dennis Smith, father and son, together at last.

Contents

Chapter 1: "The day I found out Elvis was My Daddy"
Chapter 2: Zona Marie
Chapter 3: I wish I'd known Elvis
Chapter 4: Coincidences? Elvis & I
Chapter 5: Music in My Blood
Chapter 6: Lawrence Welk
Chapter 7: Nashville and Aconda Records
Chapter 8: The Bloodline of my Grandparents – Gladys & Vernon
Chapter 9: Stories on the Road
Chapter 10: Heartbreak Hotel
Chapter 11: My Son
Chapter 12: Preaching the Gospel
Chapter 13: Elvis' Death and Military Flag
Chapter 14: Acknowledging and Accepting my Birthright
Chapter 15: Let the Boy Sing
Appendix
Photos

Description of Contents
(Sample Chapter)

Chapter One: The Day I found out Elvis was My Daddy

Tears like waves on an ocean swell up inside me and pour out as I remember every detail exactly as if it had just happened. Just a few days before my 27th year celebration of being brought into this world by my birth mother who had put me up for adoption I was reunited with "My Momma."

It was early June of 1988 and my amigo and close confidante, Randy H. of Texas had just helped me find my "real" birth mother after three weeks of constant dead ends. Randy had a skill with computers just as I had talent with my voice and picking guitar. Searching the "internet" was not the same then as it is now; it was much less sophisticated and not nearly a tenth of the information available to the public. After endless phone calls and hang ups, finally success as a male voice answered, "Hello."

I responded hesitantly as I had tired of rejection after failed rejection, "Is there a Zona Marie at this number?"

A long silence was my answer and then came, "Dennis, Dennis is that YOU?"

My heart pounding, the receiver and my hand shaking with voice quivering I managed to stutter a few syllables that were close to equating into words, "Uh huh, yeah, it's me, John Dennis Smith and I'm lookin' for my momma."

The next thing that happened made me break down in tears as I crumbled to my knees and wept like a child.

"Hello, Dennis, John, Johnny," came the reply or the question of whether I was of a swept away past, the lost son from Zona Marie.

We talked briefly as mumbled voices mixed with sniffs and tears filled most of the driveled conversation. Concrete plans were made through the slushy telephone call and a meeting place was determined for the 3rd of July 1988.

As I hung up the telephone I couldn't believe what my ears had just heard, "Yes, that would be lovely to meet you for dinner on your Birthday. I will see you then, take care 'til we see each other in a couple of weeks."

It was Friday afternoon and I was going to meet with Zona Marie, my momma of whom I had not seen for over eleven years and at that time I did not realize that she was "my mother." Zona Marie had been in my past, in my earlier childhood and toddler days; she had been a friend of the family is what I had always thought and then we lost touch when I began traveling with the Lawrence Welk show at the age of sixteen.

I pulled into the huge parking lot almost an hour early in anticipation of seeing my mother for literally the first time since being sent away for adoption. Mother Momma…..It would take lots of practice rolling those words off my tongue to get used to the sound of it. I stretched my neck to investigate the asphalt covered lot that was partially filled by a Piggly Wiggly Supermarket, a Kentucky Fried Chicken drive thru and a pharmacy store. My Chevy pickup truck idled roughly as I tried to limit my apprehension by listening to the radio with Glen Campbell's voice coming through the speakers as he sang his number one hit song, Like a Rhinestone Cowboy.

I wasn't dressed as nor did I look like a Rhinestone Cowboy, but rather I had taken on a bit of a George Strait look with my pressed Wranglers, my favorite blue Sunday 'go to meeting' shirt, of which I had made sure to have it heavily starched for this tremendous occasion. Yes, I was dressed extra fancy for a Friday afternoon with my best reptile (alligator) cowboy boots and my beige, felt, Resistol cowboy hat and a blue handkerchief in my pocket to help dispense of the sweat that beaded up on my forehead this humid and hot day; a day before our nation's two hundred and twelfth day of birth and freedom.

My chest was filled with tremendous pride, my stomach filled with swirling butterflies as I craned my neck and strained my eyes for all and any activity within the lot structure which also included the restaurante Papa's Italian of which my mother had suggested we meet at five for dinner and re-acquaintance on my twenty seventh birthday. Not a single person stirring nor any cars pulling into the lot. I had parked in such a way as to be able to see any cars pulling in nearby to the Italian restaurant. I glanced at the time on the big, expensive Rolex wrapped around my wrist to see how much time had passed since arriving at 4:10 pm. I looked away in disgust as only twenty minutes had ticked away. My shirt was starting to feel heavy from the constant perspiration that was eluding from my glands and into the fine cotton. My knuckles had turned white from clutching the steering wheel as I grew tenser with each passing of the second hand of the watch that my manager, H.T. had given me upon successful completion of three years performing on the Lawrence Welk Show. My Lawrence Welk career had ended, it had served as a training ground for my Nashville career which was about to begin at the age of eighteen. H.T. had agreed to become my manager and had given me the watch as a gift and as a memento to our friendship and business agreement of which both still hold true to this day. My manager and friend certainly wasn't the biggest fan of this meeting and journey I was about to embark upon. He had warned, "There'd be uncomfortable secrets here."

"Was Zona Marie full of those secrets that H.T. had warned of?" I thought quietly to myself.

"What the heck was wrong with the air conditioning in this truck," I snarled as I ran my fingers along the collar of my neck to ease the tension. I raised my arm to smell the arm pit underneath to make sure my deodorant was working overtime. I wondered if my birth mother was all about cleanliness and baths the way Etta, my adoptive mother had been. That is, before she passed away and was laid to rest beside my music loving adoptive dad, I.D. Smith. The memory of both of my adoptive parents being taken from me made me want to cry; but, suddenly I remembered that I would soon be meeting and hugging my "real" mother in a matter of minutes and starting a new chapter in my life. With a tightened jaw and pulled back shoulders I inhaled a deep breath of confidence mixed sparingly with bravery and joy.

The restaurant that had been suggested by Zona Marie was near her home as I had been the one who had driven a few hundred miles for this mother – son rendezvous. It was very plain from the outside except for having the three Italian flag colors of red, green and white painted smartly around the front door entrance. It seemed a decent enough place; however, I would have expected a little more exotic location and name as Papa's Italian in the deep south just didn't quite fit well. One thing was clear, my mother must not have a great deal of money as I had suspected from the start. I didn't have much dinero either, at least not like I did when I was one of Nashville's hottest young stars as H.T. and others had bestowed upon me. Those times in Nashville seemed like a lifetime and a half ago.

The door of Papa's was too far away for me to be able to read the sign hanging there. I tried to imagine it welcoming, "Birth Mother and her long, lost adopted Son." My being early had not helped me cruise over the thoughts of having not seen Zona Marie for more than a decade. I hadn't seen her; but, perhaps she had seen me through the Stetson hat crowds. Maybe, she had peeked in on me a time or two while I was performing as I am now pretty sure I had spotted her a couple times as part of the listening and clapping audience. I was hoping that she had seen me perform and had smiled when hearing my music.

I exhaled heavily, sending a cloud of thin dust airborne from the sun faded dashboard.

Was that her? At the far end of the parking lot, a lady with black hair twirled two feet high was pushing a cart from the supermarket. She looked as if she was about the age I imagined my mother looking. No, it wasn't her; she unloaded the bags from her shopping cart into the car, settled into the driver's seat and vanished just like my momma had done twenty five years or so ago. "Momma," I said aloud to the miniature pocket bible sitting next to me, sitting stately, quietly as if on a pew listening to a solemn sermon.

"Momma." Maybe if I said it a few more times or practiced writing this special word down, just maybe, it wouldn't feel so strange saying it. Zona Marie was not the momma who'd sent me back to the washroom if she'd suspected I hadn't washed my hands before eating. She was not the momma who'd walked me every day to my Christian school and had watched over me while I did my homework and then afterwards rewarded me with peach pie. I thought of all those past memories, all those things I had done before I went on the road at age nine. I had grown up too quickly because of music and life on the road.

No, this momma had missed out on all the fond memories I had of my adopted mother. I wondered if the momma I was about to meet wished she'd been there with me during those childhood years.

I ran the palms of my hand over my eyes slowly and distinctly to get a handle on my running emotions. "Do not," I scolded myself, "do not cry." I did not want the woman who delivered me into someone else's hands when I was sixteen months to see any sadness or regret from me. I am sure she has a difficult enough time already without me adding to her agony or self blame.

I looked at my time piece wrapped snugly around my wrist, "only five more minutes," I quietly mumbled. Another eligible lady age wise was now in sight; she a blonde with a roundish figure, however there were three children with her and Zona Marie had promised it would be her only at our meeting. Oh, how I hoped she hadn't lost her nerve and decided once again that she didn't want me in her life. Once again, I felt as if I were a helpless child, a little kid without a mother. I hadn't felt this alone and scared in some twenty odd years or maybe in all my life. Perhaps I did once, no, I don't believe that time ......

Wait! Was that her? A mini skirted woman much too sexy for me to freely call "momma" stepped from the convertible. I slid, slinking slowly into my vinyl seats and followed her uncovered, sleek legs to the restaurant door. No, that just couldn't be her, she hadn't looked around, she walked with too much confidence and purpose to be joining a son that had been lost for years.

Five minutes after five. Zona Marie wasn't too late, not yet. I turned the ignition off and clenched the steering wheel until my hands ached. I looked at my watch once more. Eight minutes past.

I'd wait another half hour, or maybe another hour. Yes, I'd wait until dark, perhaps I'd wait the rest of my life. I wanted to see my momma, I needed to see my momma. "Get a grip, you hear!" I commanded myself as I could feel sickness wheeling itself upon and into the lower body of my stomach and an unfamiliar ache arise. A great many of things could have happened to slow a forty seven year old mother down. Maybe the regret had been too much for her, maybe I should not have tried contacting her. Had I disrupted her life? Was she content? Had she forgotten about me like an old book? These questions and more gushed at me like a raging, non forgiving river of no return.

Surely, she would come, she'd made an effort after all. Otherwise, I wouldn't have found that pile of unopened letters hidden away in my sister's drawer, letters addressed to me.

I rolled down the Chevy's window. I needed to breathe, I needed more room for my fears, more space for feelings that I had never experienced.

I had spent weeks puzzling out where Zona Marie lived, and weeks before that questioning if I should indeed search for my birth mother. I had been successful at squeezing information from sentimental clerks and skirting around local privacy rules. I had been better at this than I was at maneuvering my way through a crowd at a concert.

Eleven minutes. The scorching heat waves rising from the black tar of the asphalt convinced me to leave the truck and walk to the entrance of Papa's Italian. "It would be better to wait on her inside if she showed," I corrected myself, "when she shows up."

I could see my reflection in the windows of the restaurant as I hiked across the heat soaked parking lot. The door felt heavy as I tugged at it and finally swung it wide as I stepped inside, making a much louder entrance than intended. I was welcomed immediately by the sound of Frank Sinatra, the smell of garlic and the feel of conditioned air. "May I take a window seat over there," I pointed to a red, vinyl booth as I asked the thin man acting as host in his white shirt and black formal pants covered in the front by an apron of red. I followed the escort with menu in hand.

Just before reaching the booth I literally froze in space. Seated at a table across from the booth where I had chosen to sit, a woman leaned forward trying to peer out the window, searching, searching for someone on the other side of the glass. She had black hair neatly tucked into a flawless roll. Her dress was of purest yellow cloth, the fabric lay dignified on uplifted shoulders. I couldn't help myself from continuing to her table. She was nervous as I noticed one of her hands caressing the fingers of the other hand.

"Mom?"

I could see the faint beginning of gray splashing through her hair. That was new, a person does change in more than a decade; I knew I had. I studied her face for the briefest of seconds as I was afraid to stare too long at her face; I did not want to make her feel uncomfortable. I looked away at the glass of half empty water in front of her on a white table cloth.

"Dennis? Johnny?" she partially questioned and half stated.

I almost lost it right there. I hadn't expected her to use my old stage name; but, maybe John Dennis, or simply John or Dennis as her husband had done when speaking on the phone. I simply was not prepared for "Johnny." My face reddened. "Mom." I repeated myself, but this time it seemed more like a relief word that I had kept bottled up inside me for an eternity. "I'm so sorry I made you wait; I, I should have come in earlier to check." I was surprised I'd been able to put together a full sentence.

"No matter," she said. "I walked through these doors an hour early. I couldn't stand to wait at home. Thought I could calm myself a bit and get used to the surroundings." Sitting too long in the same place, she shifted her seating position. She continued, "I wanted to practice what I would say to you." Her glance met the swinging door that led to the kitchen. "The waitress must have thought I was crazy, mumbling to myself."

"Naw, lots of people talk to themselves, I do it all the time. Most of the time I sing to myself. And not too quietly."

Her smile went completely into her eyes. "I've never known you to sing quietly."

Instantly, I remembered that smile, that life in those eyes. I felt my whole body begin to relax. "I'm even louder now, and sometimes I move to a corner where all can see me."

"I know," her voice simmered.

Strange that my singing story was the first thing I had chosen to tell my mother about myself. I wasn't the most modest child a momma may have wanted. I was a ham and I hoped she would still accept my love for her. Those green eyes that are shaped very much like mine and her pinched rose lips and the way she'd touch her skirt as if pressing it, and, and ...... I wanted to hug my mother, to tell her how much I loved her, to tell her it didn't matter to me that she gave me up for adoption. I was truly happy at that moment.

"Can I get you two something to drink?" asked the impatient waitress as she tapped her pen against the light green order pad. "We got a Cabernet that's real good."

I wanted something hard to drink, but was afraid Zona Marie might have a negative opinion when it came to liquor. I could order some sweet tea, manage to drink it if she ordered tea, or just stick with ice water, or even a glass of milk to appear as I took much better care of my body than what I really did.

Zona Marie looked over to the bar where the booze lined up against the long mirror. Yes, this was more like it. I was warming up to my old home state of Louisiana.

"Seagram's 7," we both announced at the same instance. We looked at each other and chuckled lightly although the waitress did not seem amused. Yes, this was indeed, truly, honestly, my momma. O Sole Mio sang by the famous tenor Luciano Pavarotti filled the air, serene.

After our salads and pastas arrived, conversation was general and easy, as we discussed the weather, my driving trip over from Texas and other non important issues. But, after our third round of drinks the talk became more personal and of memories we had of each other when I had thought she just a visiting friend of the family. We talked of the very few holidays we had shared, an occasional concert where she had attended, but had not talked or met with me, just listened to me sing and then scurried off into her world so as not to disrupt either of our lives. We shared our likes, our dislikes. Uncannily, we found were very similar in our tastes in music especially. We discussed how overrated Eddy Raven was, how much we adored How Great Thou Art, and how neither of us cared much for Madonna's onstage antics as well as being very nit picky about pop music as a music genre.

As Zona ate, I watched her twirl and wind noodles around her fork until she had room to add no more. She suddenly said, "I never stopped loving you."

Warmth filled my complete being. "Me too."

"Forgive" was never mentioned that day. "Forgive" was not a word we used that day. "Forgive" was not needed. I felt as if I were in a dream of which I prayed I would not be woken from. I was here with "My Mother," just her and me. No one else in the world mattered.

That afternoon we stayed at the table as if we were an Italiano Familia celebrating an event such as a new addition to the family. As much as we ate, neither of us finished our spaghetti and meatballs. Etta and I.D. would have scolded and made me finish my plate. But, my momma didn't scold as she hadn't finished hers either. Life was grand.

Now that the meal was at a close, I asked mother, "How's Buddy doing?" I wasn't sure whether to ask the question or not but I did want to know if he had come back into her life after she gave me and my two older sisters away to strangers. He had stayed separated from Zona Marie even after she had gotten pregnant, probably the reason she had set us free for adoption. Three babies barely out of diapers were too much for a young woman to care for on her own. I felt uncomfortable being of the same blood and genes of this man for this reason. "Ever see him?" "Was that him that answered the telephone?"

She tensed up, stared down at the table, held her breath for such a length of time that I started breathing for her as it looked as if her lungs would explode.

Why in the hell had I brought up Buddy. I didn't care about Buddy, not the way he had left my mother with two baby girls and another child on the way. I believed that he and Zona had divorced soon after our adoption, but I wasn't for sure. I had wondered if somehow they had gotten back together, had talked about missing different things with my sisters such as their first high school dances or maybe they had talked of me and what paths of life I might have taken.

"That was long ago done," she whispered, sounding as if she had just been beaten to within an inch of her life. She looked up at me with sorrow and less dignity than what had been exuding from her just minutes past.

Our eyes locked and her pupils consumed the emerald of her eyes. She leaned slightly toward me as if she wanted to tell me something, something horrible, something traumatic. Something that I most likely did not want to hear. My heart increased its beatings, its pounding, making its way up my chest into my head until all I could hear was pounding. Thud, thud, thud…. all I could feel was the thunder of my entire body ready to quake open at any moment.

Zona opened her mouth to speak, but the kitchen door swung open at that same instance and the waitress followed simultaneously. She untied and threw her apron into a booth near us in one smooth motion. As she moved to the door with keys jingling, she touched switches that dimmed the lighting of the dining room. I looked at my watch, it was nearly 11:00 pm, we had been eating, had been talking for nearly six hours. Why did this gal need to be in such a rush, couldn't she tell that I was getting to know my momma? But, on the other hand something about her demeanor told me maybe she didn't care about her momma, or perhaps her momma was no longer alive. I decided not to say anything, instead I grabbed on tight to my napkin, pulled four twenties from my wallet and laid it next to the bill.

I didn't want to leave just yet and this maneuver gave us a little more precious time as the "I wanna get the hell outta here and home" waitress made change.

Zona Marie took my fist that had the balled up napkin in it and held it in hers. "Johnny," my real momma spoke clearly and with tears in her eyes, "Elvis was your daddy."

Chapter Two: Zona Marie

Who is Zona Marie? This will probably be the second most asked question that will be posed once I finish writing and start promoting this autobiography about "The Son of Elvis Presley."

Most importantly, Zona Marie is my biological mother, MY MOTHER! Zona Marie played a very small part in my life along the periphery of when I was growing up and being raised by Elvis's Uncle I.D. and Aunt Etta.

Zona Marie was a lover and cousin by marriage to Elvis and bore his child of whom they named John Dennis Smith.

Zona Marie was the recipient of whom the song that Elvis recorded in 1961 was about and named for. "(Marie's the Name)" of His Latest Flame" is a song recorded in a hit version by Elvis Presley and published by Elvis Presley Music in 1961. The hit song performed well on both pop and easy listening stations, reaching #4 on the Billboard Top 100, and #2 on the Easy Listening chart, based (at the time) on the Top 100;

At the age of twenty six I located my mother. On my twenty seventh birthday I was reunited with my birth mother, Zona Marie, in South Louisiana. Over the course of our private meetings, I discovered many uncanny connections between my mother and me, including having many friends and acquaintances in common. She'd written to me over the years, but I'd never received the letters. I now have a bagful of those hidden birthday cards and photographs dated from the early sixties to today. She told me the amazing secret of my birthright. Elvis Presley was my daddy; I was a love child conceived during three passionate days and nights in November of 1960.

Chapter Three: I wish I had known Elvis

My Daddy, Elvis Presley, the King of Rock 'n' Roll died a young man and well before he should have. I would have loved to have known this man, this legend as a friend and as a son.

I was not a part of my Daddy's daily life, but Elvis did keep an eye on me from my birth as he and his friend and singer Sherrill Neilson were at the Hidalgo Hospital in Edinburgh, Texas when I was born premature. Elvis had been on set filming "Wild in the Country" when he received word that Zona Marie had been rushed to the hospital and was due to give birth early. Being the caring and nurturing human being that Elvis was, he had left the set and with his close companion and confidante and had arrived in Edinburgh disguised, as to not bring an unwanted media frenzy to the border town in the south of Texas.

Even though I did not know Elvis as my daddy, I had met Elvis as he held me when I was a toddler of which I have the photo. I was given a birthday card signed by Elvis and Sherrill given to me in Nashville, Tennessee.

Elvis and I.D. had instructed H.T. to keep an eye on me at the age of eleven and true to his word to Elvis, H.T. has been and remained a positive role model, manager and most importantly a true friend.

Chapter Four: Coincidences? Elvis & I

Both Elvis and I appeared and performed on the Louisiana Hayride almost 20 years apart.

In 1954, a special 30-minute portion of Louisiana Hayride was being broadcast every single Saturday on the AFN Pacific channel of the United Kingdom Scottish Forces Radio Network. On October 16th of that year, a little known teenager named Elvis Presley from Memphis, Tennessee appeared on the radio program. On March 3, 1955, Elvis made his first television appearance on the TV version of the program, carried by KSLA-TV.

I began singing at age two. At age twelve, almost twenty years later, I too had appeared on the Louisiana Hayride, winning in three categories of the talent search contest, and later was invited and played there as a special guest. I have been fortunate to also appear several times on the Grapevine Opry near Fort Worth, Texas. Also, another interesting note is that my adopted father, I.D. Smith, sang first tenor in the Deep South Quartet on the Louisiana Hayride.

I had sang along with the radio hundreds of times to The Green, Green Grass of Home trying to harmonize with my boyhood idol Mr. Tom Jones who was a great friend of my Daddy Elvis.

Elvis Aaron Presley and I had many more things in common than just the love of music and entertaining at similar venues. Yes, Elvis believed and I believe in charity, that of helping those less fortunate when the opportunity arises and we are in the financial position to do so. Women; my Daddy and I have a strong weakness for beautiful women. But, for all the less fortunate commonalities we were both blessed with spirituality. We both collected badges (symbols of heroism protection). We both loved having and collecting our guns (both of us having earned marksmen). We both quickly earned great success, entertained in many of the same places, and each of us had strong-willed managers who guided our lives and careers closely. Elvis had the Colonel. I had HT. It was as if the genetic connection between me and my father was magic. Sadly, Elvis and I also both lost our sons because of outside forces and individuals taking control of our lives.

Chapter Five: Music in My Blood

I am my father's son. Musical talent exuded from the blood in my veins even from the young age of two as I began singing just shortly after learning to talk. My voice was unusually strong for my age when I was four-years-old. Juilliard School of Music inducted me into its halls twice by the time I had turned nine. I was rebellious even then and didn't care to sing the classical pieces required. My preferences instead were Pistol Packin' Mama, Ding Dong Daddy from Dumas and of course my favorite The Green Green Grass of Home. I didn't care for the classical style that was expected of me to perform. That style just didn't quite work with my personality. It wasn't long before I moved on.

The great Eddy Kozak was commissioned to teach me at the age of ten, the art of music. Eddy moved from Chicago to Shreveport (where he'd met his wife Marjorie) for the warmer climate as he saw the lukewarm temperature of pop give way to the rising heat and popularity of rock and roll. In Shreveport, he quickly built a reputation as "Mr. Music," opening a studio where he taught an estimated 20,000 students over a 50+year of teaching career of which I was a part of. Eddy Kozak gave me all of three lessons before telling my parents they could save their money because I already played the guitar better than he did.

Chapter Six: Lawrence Welk

The headlines of the Shreveport Journal's "Weekend" edition on Friday, May 2nd, 1980 read: "It's been two years since the kid from Shreveport, John Dennis Smith walked up on stage during a Lawrence Welk concert at Hirsh Memorial Coliseum and sang the classic song Green, Green Grass of Home. This song was one of my all time favorites to sing and was written by Claude "Curly" Putman, Jr. and first recorded by singer Johnny Darrell. It is a country song originally made popular by Porter Wagoner in 1965, where it reached #4 on the country chart. It was sung later by Tom Jones in 1966 where it reached #1 in the UK Singles Chart on December 3rd and staying there for a total of seven weeks. I had heard it on the radio several times by my idol Tom Jones who just happened to be a great friend of my Daddy Elvis. I sang to an audience of 8000 persons and since that time I've appeared on various Welk shows, toured Hawaii and recorded three albums.

It was a cold windy day in March 1978 when I had accompanied my aunt to the concert. Lawrence Welk had invited members of the audience to dance with his band members; but, I wasn't interested in dancing. I wanted to sing. Mr. Welk was quite surprised and caught off guard by my request but allowed me, this 16- year-old student from Grawood Christian School, my turn at having the microphone.

"I really don't know why I did it," I later said in an interview a couple of years later in 1980. However, now that I look back on that moment in time, I realize exactly why I wanted to sing; it was because I had my Daddy's musical blood and soul flowing through me. Yes, I was a part of Elvis and was drawn upon that stage to perform and wanted to share my talent with the world.

Well, Mr. Welk invited me on an eight-day tour of Hawaii following that performance and I was absolutely ecstatic with the offer of becoming an overnight star with a trip to the Islands to boot. I then moved to Los Angeles area and played at the Lawrence Welk Country Club Village in Escondido, California. This country club was similar to a training program for entertainers. It was sort of a tourist attraction – a large club with golf courses and a couple of trailer parks. I remember there being a great many of retired persons attending the shows mixed in with vacationers of all ages. I was living life large and was becoming more and more in love with the stage and the beginning stages of fame.

Chapter Seven: Nashville and Adonda Records

When I turned 18 years of age I began recording on the Adonda label in Nashville which is one of the longest running and most successful labels in the United States.

Adonda Records (a subsidiary of HTi Music) was created in the early 50's by the legendary Booking Agent, Don Fowler. He named the label after his daughter, Donna, whose life was suddenly taken from this earth by a drunk driver. In the late 50's, Don Fowler and Harrison Tyner became good friends and in the mid 60's combined their talents and efforts, becoming partners in the Music Business. They continued their business association until Don suddenly passed away from a heart attack, at which time sole ownership was conveyed to Harrison. Over the years, there have been many recordings produced and released on this label, making it among the oldest surviving independent labels in Nashville. The label has produced world famous recording artists such as Ray Walker, The Jordanaires, and Sherrill Nielsen. In the early eighties I was the new kid on the block, the chosen new recording artist and the label's hottest brand in Nashville, Tennessee and became the toast of the town. H.T. (Harrison Tyner) had become my manager at the handshake of my adopted dad, I.D. Smith with Don Fowler present. The three of them were on a fishing trip with Don Baker as their guide.

My future in Nashville had been set and determined in a relaxed atmosphere at Sam Rayburn Lake in east Texas.

Chapter Eight: The Bloodline of my Grandparents – Gladys & Vernon

I remember meeting my Grandpa on my Daddy's side when I was six years old; but, unfortunately my Paternal Grandmother had passed on three years before I was to be brought into this world. However, I do have a precious memento of My Grandmother in my possession; on this memento is her thoughts and wishes.

To fully understand where I fit into the Presley brood, I will begin the writing and telling of Elvis' and my family lineage.

Elvis' Father – Vernon Elvis Presley was born on April 10th, 1916 in Fulton, Mississippi to Jesse (1896-1973) and Minnie Mae Hood, 'Grandma Dodger' Presley (1890-1980). Elvis' Mother - Gladys Love Smith was born on April 25th, 1912, in Pontotoc County, Mississippi to Bob (1873-1931) and Doll Smith (1876- 1935).

Gladys' mother, 'Doll' Smith died fairly young at age 59 in 1935 and was buried next to her husband Bob Smith, both in unmarked graves. So like Elvis, Gladys lost her mother at a young age. Gladys was 23, Elvis 22.

When my Grandfather Vernon started dating my Grandmother Gladys there was only one true object of his affection; that object was Gladys. Vernon was still a kid at seventeen when he married Gladys Love Smith who was four years his elder. They eloped and were married June 17th, 1933 in the County of Pontotoc, where Vernon was not known, as both newlyweds lied about their ages. Vernon gave his age as 22, Gladys 19. Gladys was of legal age; but, Vernon was not, being just 17.

Like many of our relatives before him, Vernon worked at any odd job that came along. For a while, he and Vester, his older brother, farmed together, raising corn, cotton and even had a few hogs. Later, he took a job with a federal government make - work program during the Great Depression. Next, he drove a delivery truck for a Tupelo wholesale grocer delivering goods to stores throughout northeast Mississippi. These Presley genes, passed down from generation to generation, some of which undoubtedly were inherited by the infant born in that two-room house in the hills of East Tupelo, Mississippi and the infant born a generation later in that hospital in Edinburgh, Texas.

Towards the latter part of June 1934, Gladys knew she was pregnant. Some time around four or five months along she was absolutely sure she was having twins: (1) she was quite large, (2) she felt two babies kicking and (3) there was a history of twin births on both sides of the family. Gladys was earning $2 a day at the Tupelo Garment Company, while Vernon milked cows on the dairy farm of Orville S. Bean. With $180 that he borrowed from Bean after Gladys became pregnant, Vernon began constructing their family home. They moved into their newly built home in December.

Elvis' birthplace was built by my Grandfather, Vernon, with help from my great Uncle Vester and my great Grandfather, Jessie, who lived next door in a relatively 'large' four-room house. I have visited my father's birthplace and have personal photos of it before it was later moved to Graceland.

Chapter Nine: Stories of the Road

Aunt Julie story: In 1994, my aunt Julie Clark was 91 years young and living In Galveston, Texas. She was the aunt of my 3rd wife and claimed that she drank a martini of gin or vodka every day of her life since age of 19 and stated that during all those years she had only once received a bad olive and never a bad drink.

There were eight of us including myself as we had been on tour and Aunt Julie insisted on buying our drinks as we were taking her out to dinner. I ordered what I wanted, so did Kyle Robalar as did a couple others and she abruptly stopped us and told the waiter that we were all to have a Bourbon and that it would do no good to argue as she was the one who would be paying the tab. Her exact words, "They will have bourbon, the best you have, over ice only and they will drink it." We laughed and joked the evening away as Aunt Julie kept us entertained telling us of life's hardships and joys in the early nineteen hundreds. She reminded us that she had lived and survived the great depression and how she wished she'd been younger in the sixties, a time of Woodstock.

Chapter Ten: Heartbreak Hotel

  I, too, like Elvis loved women and have had many love affairs, flings and one nighters. Yes, my love for beautiful women have gotten me into my share of trouble.

  My first real sweetheart became my wife when I was nineteen. This first marriage failed due to my life on the road. The band and I had come home early from a concert tour and I was surprising my wife with flowers and an extended stay at home with her and my son. Needless to say, I was the one surprised when I entered my home to find my "best friend" sitting in his underwear slouching in my recliner in our front room. My wife at the time was coming out of the bathroom in her negligee while my four-year-old son looked on from his vantage point on the floor.

  In disbelief at what I had witnessed, I went straight to the bedroom and pulled my 357 Magnum from its hiding place in the closet, placed in the corner above the shelf. With all the confusion of her and him trying to come up with alibis and excuses, I lost it and told him to open his mouth and I jammed the barrel of the gun in deep as he struggled to beg for his life, nearly naked and unable to speak clearly.

  My baby boy started crying and that is when I made the decision not to pull the trigger for shame had gotten the better of me. I did not want my son to have an image of the horrible blood bath his home would become. I gently squeezed the hammer back in place, while not to gently removing the piece from the cheating prick's orfice while breaking a tooth or two and left that place forever.

  Two more wives and failed marriages followed, one which was annulled. I readily admit after my first marriage I was the one propelled into affairs. These extra marital affairs played a significant role in these two breakups.

After years of womanizing, I changed my ways and married for a fourth time. Lisa and I live a humble life and we are devoted to each other today and every day that follows.

Chapter Eleven: My Son

  I was there for my son until he was four. The adulterous woman and I divorced and I found it to be a constant conflict to remain in their lives since my ex-best friend and ex-wife had tied the knot before the ink had dried on our divorce papers. Now, I look back and wish I would have fought to keep my son and raised him as I had been brought up.

  Years passed and then I received a devastating phone call one night that my son, now of seventeen years had been involved in an accident. He had been killed by a drunk driver. I called the Idaho State Police as I had received the news via a friend of my ex-mother-in-law. A State trooper verified that a teen boy had indeed been killed on that night. I wept and wept for hours upon hours. I agonized over not being there for him, of not knowing him, of not giving him the love he deserved and now would never have. A dense fog covered my life.

  Now, I had a clue as to how Elvis might have felt when he knew that he could not share his love for his only son.

  Then ten years later a miracle came to my doorstep. The young man, my son of whom I thought I had lost forever was looking for his father and at about the same age as I was when I sought my mother. A lie was now conquered by the truth, my son was alive, full of life and so was I.

Chapter Twelve: Preaching the Gospel

My famous daddy had success with gospel music because of two things: (1) Elvis had a great voice that showered reverence when he sang, (2) Most importantly, Elvis had a strong belief in GOD. When people would call Elvis "The King." he'd reply, "There's only one King," meaning our Father who art in Heaven.

I, too had a strict Christian upbringing with my adoptive parents which should come of no surprise or shock as my adoptive parents were related to Elvis' mother and dad. I.D. Smith was a music minister and a great influence on me. Our entire family was active in the Church of Christ, all singing for the congregation. I went on missions, offered testimonials and even spent time preaching and singing of GOD's praise and glory in India. I studied and spent four years of training to become an ordained minister. Today, I still have my strong belief in the Lord Jesus Christ as my Saviour and of GOD as my Heavenly Father. I consider myself as a nondenominational Christian and will enter a church every once in a while to take me back and remind me of my precious times at service during my childhood.

Like Elvis, I believe a person's work and how they treat others is more important than the hypocrisy of going to church to be seen. Also, I strongly believe in helping another man, woman or child when possible and to do it when no one else is looking or the when the good deed can go unannounced and unrecognized by others.. I and others occasionally joke about the "Gospel according to John." Ask me to sing a gospel song and I hope you'll hear the reverence for GOD in my voice.

Chapter Thirteen: Elvis' Death and Military Flag

There has long been speculation, quiet whispers and loud conversations as to why there was never an American Flag draped over Elvis' casket after his supposed and announced death on August 16, 1977. As a veteran that served his country with dignity and honorably, Elvis had the right to have a U.S. flag draped over his coffin at Forest Hill Cemetery. Whether or not his dad Vernon Presley denied it as he did mention that Elvis loved red roses and since nothing could be put atop the U.S. flag my Grandfather may have opted for the flowers instead. More than likely Elvis did not have this detail written in his will. Or.……?

I believe Elvis died in 1984 as I was awarded a flag several years after his famous funeral in August of '77.' I do believe that Elvis suffered a stroke of great magnitude and was unable to function normally and that his close friends and family felt it better to announce Elvis' death than to risk him being seen as helpless or possibly an invalid. There has been many a discussion and theory of where Elvis might have been living or where he was taken to hide him from the cameras and the public that loved him so. Some say Buenos Aires under the alias of "Jon Burrows," others theorize that Elvis was held prisoner at his own estate, the home he purchased as a gift for his family, a seclusion for he, his mother and father.

Chapter Fourteen: Acknowledging and Accepting My Birthright

Long ago in a world we only hear and read about, there was a code amongst friends, gentlemen and ladies. A code that was a bond in the form of a hearty handshake and your own given word. This was a time before contracts, a time before lawyers, a time of honor. This honorable handshake was prevalent in the West and especially in the South and this was the world Elvis had known and had grown to love and trust.

In 1960 when my mother and father had their three day love fest and the following days that the Colonel heard about it, all those close to Elvis including Sherrill "Shawn" Neilsen, Harrison Tyner, the Jordaniare backup singers to Elvis, Don Fowler, I.D. Smith, Etta Smith and of course Zona Marie were all instructed and schooled to not mention the incident and later "the son." There might have been other musicians that I had worked with that knew and or had music dealings with Elvis, that had also gave their solemn oath to not breathe a word to the media, to the public, nor to their own families. Mitch Kryrum (Elvis' private photographer) who came out of retirement at H.T.'s request to photograph me and who passed onto me never before published photos of Elvis must have known. It is a possibility that Priscilla Presley and Lisa Marie may know of my hidden story and birthright. I do not know for certainty how far the secret was buried and how many persons have been touched by the code of honor.

Chapter Fifteen: Let the Boy Sing

After being reacquainted with my momma, Zona Marie, I asked her a few months later of any proof that Elvis was my daddy. She laughed lightly and said, "My dear son, you have had the proof in your possession all along."

"I'm not talking about my musical talent, or my voice left me by the father I never knew. I'm talking proof. Something tangible that I can actually show people. Momma, I need something that can't and won't be written off as coincidental or an interesting story." Once again, she smiles and tells me that I have the proof.

"What is it?"

"You know that "Mother's poem" in the frame, the one that explains what is means to be a mom? Why is it that you have that, and I, your mother, does not? That's your proof."

"Mom, it talks about what it is to be a mother. That ain't proof?" I continued to question.

"It's what is written on the back," she playfully teases.

"There's nothing there. Just a hole where it hangs on the wall. Mom, please tell me what this is about."

"When you get home take the poem out of the frame, son. Then turn it over and read what is written on the back."

A few days later, I took the poem out of the frame and flipped it over. And there, in faded pencil, written in the hand of one of our maids, is a note from my Grandmother Presley. I can barely make out the faded words plus my hands are shaking. It mentions what it means to be a mom and it then mentions me, that if ever there is any question about who that boy is or where he comes from, "You just tell them to let the boy sing."

Appendix

Sealed Birth Certificate of John Dennis Smith showing Elvis Aaron Presley as father and Zona Marie as mother. Contrived Birth Certificate of John Dennis Smith showing I.D. Smith as father and Etta Smith as mother. DNA Test showing John Dennis Smith confirmed 99.9% as being the son of Elvis Presley. Letter from H.T. (Bill Tyner) stating that when the time is right, John Smith can let the world know that Elvis was his daddy. Various birthday cards sent that had been hidden from John Smith that were sent by his birth mother Zona Marie.

Photos

There will be twenty-to-thirty pages of photos, including the following list represented by captions:

Family photos
1. Photos of John (from birth to present)
2. I.D. Smith, tenor with the Deep South Quartet
3. John's adoptive parents
4. John's siblings
5. Photos of John and his aunts
6. Additional family photos

Photos related to John's music career
7. Adonda Records Presents Dennis Smith album cover
8. John's studio portrait
9. John Starr CD sleeve notes World, We Will Be Late Today
10. John Starr CD sleeve notes Cowboy King with quotes
11. Two photos of John and Harrison Tyner
12. Photos of Ray Walker and the Jordanaires
13. Performance photo

Elvis Photos
14. Toddler John Dennis Smith held by Elvis.
15. Preadolescent John Dennis Smith on stage with Elvis.
16. Elvis and Sherrill Nielsen on stage signed Happy Birthday John "Dennis" from Sherrill Nielsen and Elvis Presley.
17. Photo of Elvis, Priscilla, Zona Marie, Glen Campbell standing together.

18. Photos of some of the archival material and artifacts mailed as gifts to John.
19. Photo of the flag from the Rose-Neath Funeral Home.
20. Photos of items belonging to Elvis.
21. Thirteen unpublished photos of Elvis.

Other photos
22. John with Dennis Weaver with Weaver's soda can home.
23. John with plane.
24. John with boat

About the Author

John Dennis Smith was born in Edinburgh, Texas just north of the Mexico border and raised in Shreveport Louisiana. He first began singing at his church at the young age of four. His music career began as a teenager singing and winning his first contest entered at the Louisiana Hayride. John's voice created quite a stir and he was billed as "Country Music's New Kid on the Block." Lawrence Welk personally recruited John at age 16, he was the youngest singer/guitar player to join the Lawrence Welk Show. A couple of years later at 18 he was writing with a team in Nashville and recording albums with Adonda Records. John's recording of his "Cowboy King" album, a collection of western music, is in the Cowboy Music Hall of Fame in Fort Worth, Texas. "World We Will Be Late Today," was his second release on Adonda. "California Calling" and "Sure Cure for the Blues" climbed high in the late 80s and early 90s on such charts as Billboard Magazine's top 30. John's "Please Let Me Love You" reached number 3 on the Indie chart and stayed there for an amazing 17 weeks.

John was the lead singer for Southern Thunder in Texas. He has played and performed with John Denver including doing music engineering work for him as well. He has worked with actor, Dennis Weaver on the economy of ecology, "Ecolonomics." He formed Smith McMillan publishing to develop the Ecolonomics school curriculum as this is his other great pastime after music. He has written for a who's who list of famous singers. Elvis was known to warm up his fingers and cool down at the piano with gospel music. There was a spiritual element to his large body of work, even when he sang in Las Vegas. John Dennis is following in his daddy's footsteps; he favors pursuing a career rich with Christian music tied in with his Country and Popular Music. John is currently recording his next two albums in Cave Creek, Arizona, where he calls home.

Smith's collaborator, Rico Austin is an Arizona author and blogger. He has worked on other projects such as screenplays, one of which is from his best selling and award winning novel "My Bad Tequila." Rico has been published in print magazines, newspapers, and on-line magazines and won numerous writing awards including (14) for "My Bad Tequila." He has been chosen as the Author to write and represent Arizona in the "50 Authors from 50 States" Blog in 2013. Rico has given presentations and readings to high school students, to audiences at libraries and at book festivals.

Rico has won dozen of awards for his personal essays, short stories, magazine and newspaper articles and novels. Much of his writing is in a few different genres such as autobiographical, biographical, fiction, travel and children's books. He is a member of the "Arizona Authors Association" in Phoenix and of "The Society of Southwestern Authors" in Tucson. He lives in Scottsdale, Arizona and San Carlos, Sonora, Mexico.

Selected Links

1. Mayor, Joseph A. Kuehner, Jr. proclaiming April 14 as John Smith Presley day in Egg Harbor City, NJ

http://www.eggharborpilot.com/Pilot/Photos/Pages/Elvis1ml#7

2. John Dennis Smith aka John Starr singing "World, We Will Be Late Today" with comment by Bass Singer Ray Walker of legendary Jordanaires

http://www.youtube.com/watch?v=9WOq2_IEgF4

3. John Dennis Smith aka John Starr singing "Cowboy King"

http://www.youtube.com/watch?v=YfR6RciTjk0

http://www.cdbaby.com/cd/starrjohn2

4. Adonda Records with John D. Smith aka John Starr as client as well as Jordanaires, Sherrill Nielsen and Ray Walker

http://htimusic.com/Adonda_Records/Adonda_Index.pdf

*KING of Rock 'n' Roll
with his son, John Dennis Smith.*

Elvis in plane.

Elvis as a Baby on horse with shadows of
Vernon & Gladys Presley.

Blonde (don't know), Sherrill "Shaun" Neilsen,
H.T. "Bill" Tyner & Zona Marie.

ID Smith, center in white,
(John's adoptive Dad & Elvis' uncle) & the Deep South Quartet.

Personal photo of John's Daddy, Elvis.

Grave site of Gladys Smith Presley.

John at about 6 years old; before his piano recital.

Dennis Smith Signs With Welk

By RHONDA JONES
Journal Staff Writer

Dennis Smith, the 16-year-old singer-guitarist who was "discovered" by Lawrence Welk during his concert show here in March, has been hired by Welk to appear periodically on his television show next season.

The young Shreveporter, who has been singing for audiences since he was six years old, got a chance to sing at the Welk concert here and received reviews as good as the famous band leader himself.

After he sang, Welk asked Dennis to meet him at his dressing room after the show where they would discuss a contract.

A few days ago Dennis received a phone call from Welk, along with an offer to appear on the television show.

Dennis' father, I.D. Smith, told the Journal that Welk has made arrangements for him to sing, beginning July 5, with a Welk concert show in Lake Tahoe, Nev., then attend a special training session in Escandido, Calif. After this, Dennis will then be able to appear on the show.

In addition to his offer from Welk a few days ago, Dennis will have his first record released in a few days — "Green, Green Grass of Home." The flip side of the 45 rpm record is "The Answer to Your Why."

Also, Tuesday will mark the beginning of another new experience for Dennis — he will leave for Hawaii with the Youree Drive Junior High School Stage Band, which is scheduled to make eight concert appearances there.

Dennis' father said the phone at the Smith residence has not stopped ringing since Dennis sang at Welk's show in March. He said persons call to congratulate him and to find out when Dennis will go on the Welk show and when and where he will appear again locally.

Saturday night Dennis will sing for the last time in Shreveport before he takes the job with Welk. He will be at the Louisiana Hayride, where he has made several appearances in the past.

Dennis has also sung at the North Caddo Hayride in Vivian, the Grapevine Opree in Grapevine, Texas, along with singing at church services and at school.

Dennis Smith
Set for Tahoe Show

John Dennis Smith at 16 years of age joins Lawrence Welk.

DENNIS SMITH

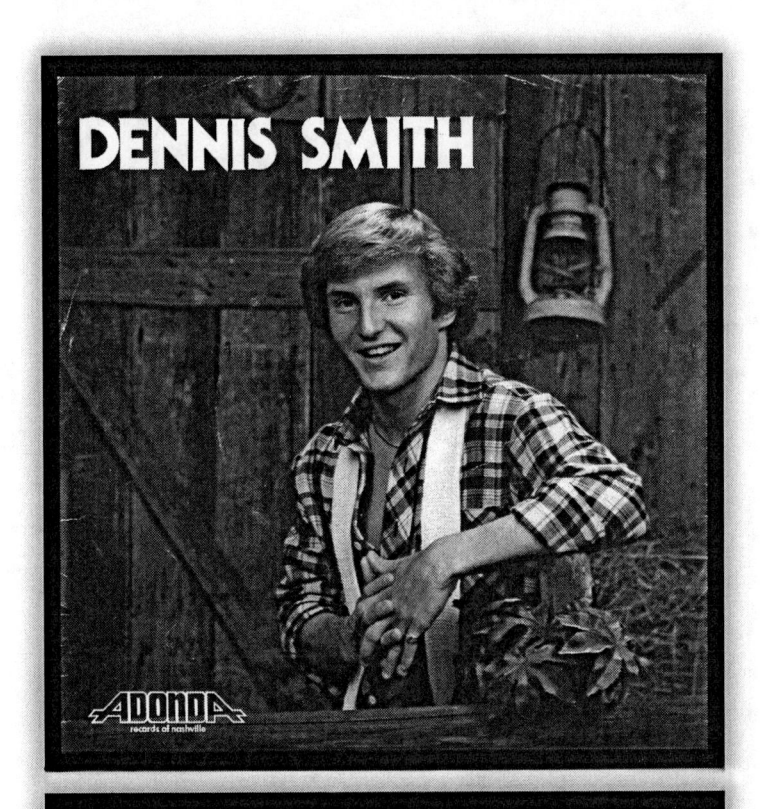

ADONDA
records of nashville

PRESENTS

DENNIS SMITH

"I think Dennis is the best singer I've found in my lifetime. As you can see, even at my age of 75 I've found this good singer and I'm in Heaven."

(Lawrence Welk, as reported in Shreveport Journal)

GET IT TOGETHER TOGETHER

"I've been very fortunate in having many of my songs recorded by some of the top stars—Elvis Presley, Dean Martin, Mickey Gilley, Frank Sinatra, Hank Williams, Jr., Eddy Arnold, to name just a few. But it was a double pleasure when Dennis Smith went into the studio for his first major recording session and recorded like he had been doing it all of his life. He did a super job on *Get It Together Together* and when you hear the cut you'll know that Dennis Smith is here to stay.

Baker Knight

CALIFORNIA CALLING

"I've written a lot of songs, some of which have been recorded by such artists as Ronnie McDowell, T. G. Shepperd, Christi Lane and Shaun Nielsen. But recently I attended Dennis Smith's recording session in Nashville and was thrilled at the depth of feeling in his singing—he certainly captured the style I had in mind when I co-wrote *California Calling*. Dennis has a real future—and that future is Music!!!"

Daniel Willis

Produced by	HARRISON TYNER and DON FOWLER	HARGUS "PIG" ROBBINS	Piano
Arranged by	HAROLD BRADLEY	HAROLD BRADLEY	Guitar
Engineered by	LES LADD	DALE SELLERS	Electric Guitar
Recorded at	WOODLAND SOUND STUDIOS	RAY EDENTON	Rhythm Guitar
	Nashville	BUDDY HARMAN	Drums
Backup Singers	JOE BABCOCK, SHAUN NIELSEN,	HENRY STRZELECKI	Bass
	LOUIS NUNLEY, HERSHAL WIGINTON	HAL RUGG	Steel

38 MUSIC SQUARE EAST, SUITE 115, NASHVILLE, TENNESSEE 37203 (615) 244-4224

In Concert

HIS DOMINION
1 CHRONICLES 29:11
TOUR

John Dennis Smith

Contemporary Christian Music With a Touch of Gospel

Concert is FREE!
(A Love Offering will be taken)

Chapter 8
The Offer?

October 16th, 2012; 8:40 am

Having boarded early on Southwest Flight 3597 from Phoenix to Oakland in Boarding Group "A" with boarding position #51 and having stowed my laptop in the overhead compartment, I had settled into a semi-comfortable aisle seat for the two hour flight into Northern California and was dozing off into a restless nod at an on time take off.

Awakened at the chime of the bell that goes off through the second rate speaker system that alerts passengers that it is now safe to walk about the cabin I looked over my notes of "Let the Boy Sing, Elvis was My Daddy" and began contemplating the last paragraph of the proposal which is, "I took the poem out of the frame and flipped it over. And there, in faded pencil, written in the hand of one of our maids, is a note from my Grandmother Presley to my birth mother. I can just make out the faded words plus my hands are shaking. It mentions what it means to be a mom and how my Grandma Presley knows what my mother is experiencing. It then mentions me, that if ever there is any question about who that boy is or where he comes from, "You just tell them to let the boy sing."

Did Gladys Smith Presley have a premonition? She was known to have seen things before they happened, the most famous of such was the fear of losing her son Elvis to fame as she had to share him with the world and eventually the fame did indeed lead to his death through overdosing of drugs to help him deal with the lack of sleep and other insecurities that a life on the road created. Gladys Presley knew that Elvis secretly loved Zona

Marie and perhaps she realized that it was just a matter of time before she bore him a male child. Gladys had not shared the poem with Zona Marie, it had been shared with her after Glady's death through the maid that had once cared for Elvis and had now cared for his biological son, John Dennis Smith.

Again, I tried to push myself to be at I.D. and Etta Smith's house during this time and imagined me being the picture frame and its contents. An incredible act of trust given an older Negro woman, employee and friend. This steadfast woman named Hattie, giving a cherished keepsake to a much younger white woman, knowing that this young woman had delivered a bastard son out of wedlock and had given all three of her children up for adoption. This servant woman kept this secret, promise and allegiance to her former employer when the time came for her to leave and care for young John at Elvis's request. Zona Marie had asked Hattie the maid to give the picture and it's frame with the message on the back to John as a keepsake whenever he was old enough to leave home.

The captain's voice came over the plane's intercom system and jolted me from Memphis and Shreveport of yesteryear back into the present. I peered out the window and took in the picturesque bay area from the air. I was scheduled to work all week visiting distributors, working with outside salespersons and performing a couple of proper tire repair seminars in the San Francisco Bay area. I had scheduled a book signing with owner Julio B. at Tommy's Mexican Restaurant in the Richmond District of San Fran for Wednesday evening during and after his weekly Tequila class. I had taken a jaunt north to Santa Rosa and then east over to Sacramento and was back in the heart of San Francisco.

October 19th, 2012;
Shopping, inspecting and looking at all the sweatshirts, memorabilia, shot glasses, I stroll merrily along the clothing business side of Fisherman's Wharf. I smile at the sun, at the sidewalk, at the tourists and the shopkeepers, it is a glorious day. "Augh, ouch, what the ....?" I look at my bare arm.

The day was warm, an untypical day in San Francisco for late October, I had opted to wear a short sleeve shirt. It was the only short sleeve shirt I had packed as I expected much cooler and brisk weather. I had walked across the Golden Gate Bridge the evening before and was amazed at the bicycles that crossed and ignored the signs that the riders and their bicycles should be on the other side. At regular intervals during my stroll I became terrified of the heights and had to remind myself that I was on a safe structure; I had always heard that the railings were higher to dissuade any thoughts of suicide as the chore would be much too difficult. But somewhere along the lines of gossip, this tale was just that. It would have been the easiest of tasks for an individual with mental problems or for an individual without mental disorders to abruptly go to the railing and ease oneself over the side, dropping, sailing and then splattering unto the hard, cold waters of the Pacific Ocean. I nervously backed myself away from the giant gerts of orange mixed with red as I noticed a man that looked to be in his late twenties or early thirties staring intently as he moved in my direction with long strides. He wore a blue jacket and a white hat like a captain of a ship would wear. His face looked dark as if it hadn't been shaved for several days and he looked as if his lips hadn't turned upward in the smile position in years. He seemed to have slight bruises spread about, near the eyes, and below his cheeks. I tried to appear as if I hadn't noticed him staring at me. I started jogging away from him. After about 100 yards of fairly brisk running I slowed and then stopped next to two couples taking pictures and looked back over my shoulder. He wasn't there or I couldn't see him. I continued my trek across the two mile span of steel; but felt as if I was being watched or followed by something or someone sinister.

Back safely to my car, I drove directly to the hotel and took a hot, relaxing shower. While letting the warm water beat down on my head and run down my entire body and vanish into the drain, I relived the moments of seeing the man on the bridge. The more I thought about it, the more I was sure that I had seen that same guy before. "Where was it, where had you seen him before," I searched my memory bank for answers. "Ah ha, he was at the book signing at Tommy's. Yes, that was it, that was the weirdo that came up to me," I said aloud to myself. He had come up to me at the bar, looked me directly in the eyes and said menacingly, "So you're the one that wrote that book, huh." Before I could respond, he had turned to walk away, I then heard him say something about "transvestite" and he was gone out the front door. This stranger vanished out into the dark night, into the streets of San Francisco.

I hadn't given it much more thought until now. "What did this character want with me? Hopefully, it was just an odd coincidence that he was on the bridge today. He wouldn't be following me? For what reason? Rico, shake it off, you're just being paranoid," I continued to talk with myself as I tried to sort this thing through. "Remember, people that are paranoid, are paranoid for a reason," I fought back with an answer to myself as me, myself and I were all in this together and we needed an explanation.

Refreshed, I was ready to stroll down to Fisherman's Wharf since I was in the neighborhood staying at the Marriott on Columbus Avenue. Just as I was opening the door of my hotel room, a ring came from my cell phone. I let the door close as I stepped back into the room as I saw the call was from John Smith. "Hello Amigo, what's up?"

"Are you sitting down? John asked excitedly.

"No, wait a second, okay, I'm seated. Is this good news?" I asked hopefully.

"Amigo, I just hung up the phone with Jane Dystel and she told me that she loves your proposal and that a publisher has offered 1 point 5 million dollars ($1.5 million) for our story!" he gushed.

"Oh my, oh my!" was all I could get out as I started to feel my eyes blurring with wet drops of tears. After fifty two years of struggling on Earth, my dreams were about to become true. I was going to be semi-rich and my writing would be read by thousands. I thanked GOD silently, then thanked John not so silently and then took a walk down to Fisherman's Wharf with the biggest grin on my face and the largest glow in my heart.

"Augh, ouch, what the ….?" I had felt this painful sensation one other time; but, it had been my big toe that was on the receiving end of a scorpion's tail, hid deep in my shoe on the back patio in Arizona. I couldn't believe the sting, the pain on my left arm in front of the elbow joint, in the area where a nurse had taken my blood for an annual checkout just months before. I looked at my arm that had just the slightest drop of blood and then at the crowd. The only thing that seemed to stand out was a thin man in a white skipper's hat with blue brim moving decidedly and quickly away from me. I saw him remove his hat and he was lost in the crowd. This human donned a blue jacket, was of slender build and looked as if he were a performer who had done an act or two of "Captain and Tenille." It was the same guy I had seen on the bridge.

October 20th, 2012; Early morning, somewhere around 4:30 am;

Awakened early by the dimming chime of my cell phone, recollection is quite clear to the eve before as my left arm is sore and a bit enflamed. "Nothing to worry about," I chided as I scrubbed ferociously at the wound, hoping that soap and water would do the same miraculous job it had done on me as a youth when I had been caught cursing with swear words for the first time. This same combo had entered my mouth to awash the shame and evil words from my vocabulary and had worked quite well as a deterrent for years during my youth.

After I dropped off my rental car, I rolled up the sleeve of my shirt to steal a glance at my arm. "It doesn't look that bad, just a slight scratch, nothing to worry about." Airport security secured me through and I boarded the plane headed back to the place I call home.

As I sat in my seat, I wrote and I tried to make sense of what had happened. I played over and over in my head of what the psychopath had said at the Mexican restaurant, "So you wrote this book" and "transvestite." I scratched my head as I tapped out words from the keyboard of my laptop, trying to figure out what was going on and then it hit me. "He was referring to pages 17 – 24 in Chapter 1 of 'My Bad Tequila,' where I'm describing the encounter with what I first believe is a woman that ends up being a man – a transvestite. Oooh, I'm freaking out! Was that guy, was he a transvestite? Was he gay?" My head was swimming in a current and my brain was struggling to stay afloat. "Is schizophrenia something that a normal person would try to hide?" Or, "If I were truly paranoid would I try to change the subject from what I originally was writing, onto something completely different to cover the depth of what I really knew to be true?" I took a deep breath, inhaled completely, exhaled deeply, and again as I told myself, "You need to calm down, quit letting your mind race down the wrong track, relax." I was starting to feel a wee bit better and then, "Does that prick have AIDS? Is he carrying the HIV virus? Why was he after me? All I did was write a story. I have friends that are gay. I wasn't gay bashing or transvestite bashing, just telling a story like it happened, nothing more. What the hell? Oh, please dear LORD, help me," I screamed throughout my body, but not a sound was heard on the plane.

October 20th, 2012; 9:20 am

"Welcome to Phoenix, thank you for choosing Southwest Airlines, we know that you have a choice and we do appreciate your traveling with us. If Phoenix is your final destination, welcome home and travel safe on the highway, if not, then check at the gate or the nearest monitor for your connecting flight." I breathe lightly as I am thankful to be home.

Unloading the tools and luggage from my trunk is when I became aware of weariness eroding itself upon and of me. Perhaps, it would have been wiser for me to have gone to the hospital immediately after "the needle jab." Instead I had elected to go celebrate the news of the grand offer. Within a matter of just a few minutes my life had gone from being on cloud nine to possibly being six feet under. My thought process had been enjoy life, this is your moment, don't let that sick, son of a bitch take it away. And so I had hailed a taxi instead and told the driver to drop me off at 16th and Guerrero.

The Elixir, in the Mission District is well known in the bay area both by drinkers and teetotalers because of its historic value as the 2nd oldest saloon in San Francisco. I knew of the Elixir for a different reason other than it being established in 1858. A classmate of mine from grad school, Thunderbird School of Global Management (T-Bird), H. Joseph E. aka H. is a partner and operates this neighborhood bar of classic San Francisco architecture. I wanted to go to a place where I knew the bartenders. Michael or Shay would be serving. H. was always wandering in and out during the evenings and would without fail on my past visits offer me a double shot of Azunia Tequila as I had helped familiarize him with that brand of tequila. My friend Jim R. of San Clemente had been the distributor and the rest is history. Yes, I wanted to be in a place where I could celebrate with a few people I knew. Gary Portnoy wrote it best, "Sometimes you want to go where everybody knows your name and they're always glad you came." Yes, in San Francisco, the Elixir was my "Cheers."

"Hi Hon, glad you're home, I can't believe the news you told me over the phone about the book deal. I am so proud of you, knew you could do it and you were able to show the literary agent what a great writer you are," greeted Connie to me.

I gave her a quick kiss, told her I needed to take a nap before going to the concert to meet John and Lisa in Cave Creek at the arena where the 'run with the bulls' event was being held. John would be singing with his band Southern Thunder and I needed again to hear his Elvis like voice to remind me of why I was involved in things of which I should have not been included.

We met up with our amiga Diana, who was one half of a couple of whom we had met in San Carlos a few years earlier. They lived in Cave Creek and she met us early that afternoon. She had parked her car in the lot between Buffalo Chip and Harold's and hopped in our SUV for front row parking that awaited us at Hogs and Horses Arena owned by another amigo, TC.

The running of the bulls didn't help me control my nerves; just the opposite as three different ambulance rides were taken by victims that chose to defy common sense and the odds. Chances are if you mess with a bull, you may get the horn.

It was good to see John and his band getting ready for the concert. John got us both margaritas and raised a toast, "To the $1.5 million book deal," and we drank. I had to smile, yes a lifelong dream of being a well known author with a bit of cash was about to become a reality. Knowing this, did help in simmering the nightmare of what might lie ahead from the previous night.

> October 21st, 2012;
> From: Rico Austin
> Subject: RE: Proposal - Let the Boy Sing, Elvis was my Daddy
> To: "John D Smith" "Jane Dystel"
> Date: Sunday, October 21, 2012; 10:33 am
> Hello Jane,

Is it possible for the 3 of us to speak together tomorrow, Monday morning? Do You have conference call ability? If not then I could meet John we could be on Speaker phone. The best number to reach me on is (480) --- ----; I look forward to speaking with You as I have a few questions I would like to ask and get Your opinions and any advice.

Gracias & Best Regards, rico

Below is the list of questions I had for Jane Dystel of which I was never able to ask due to the offer not materializing. I shared this list with John.

Questions to Jane about publisher's offer:
1. What is or are the risks of countering an offer?
   a. Counter at perhaps $1,500,000 & 10% of total sales after breakeven point at 250,000 copies or whatever that number may be; Tie offer into success of book;
   b. If counter offer is not accepted then what? Will original offer still be on table?
2. How many publishers has the proposal been sent to?
3. Who is the publisher with the now standing offer?
4. How will we be paid! I know 15% to Jane Dystel Co. & then 50/50 split to John / Rico as per verbal agreement and handshake on Oct. 15th, 2012; How is it distributed? Is it half now & half later?
5. What kind of timeline are we looking at? How many months to finish project?
6. Will there be chapter time lines or how often do I send my work to publisher for critique / approval?
7. Do we stay quiet on this project or are we allowed to discuss on social media such as Facebook, Twitter &/or Blog?
8. Do we keep full movie rights to the book?

How are pictures sent? Some are one of a kind – valuable and sentimental; What kind of security measures and procedures to insure John gets them back after they have been scanned for book?

October 21st, 2012;
From: Jane Dystel
Subject: RE: Proposal - Let the Boy Sing, Elvis was my Daddy
To: "Rico Austin" "John D Smith"
Cc: "Miriam Goderich"
Date: Sunday, October 21, 2012; 11:27 am
Rico,

It is Miriam's turn to read the proposal and she won't have a chance to read it this weekend. Let's save your questions until after we have finished doing this and can get back to you.

Thank you for being in touch.

Jane

Jane Dystel
Dystel & Goderich Literary Management
One Union Square West Suite 904
New York, NY 10003 www.dystel.com
(Ph) 212 --- ----, ext. 12 (Fax) 212 --- ----

This would be the next to last email of which I received from Jane. According to John, "Jane had sent him one more email saying that the offer had been rescinded due to partner Miriam Goderich not approving the proposal." The last email I would receive from Jane nearly a month later stated to me that Dystel and Goedrich were not interested in handling "My Bad Tequila," even though, to my knowledge, no one in their organization had ever read it. I was turned away from even mailing a copy for possible evaluation or representation.

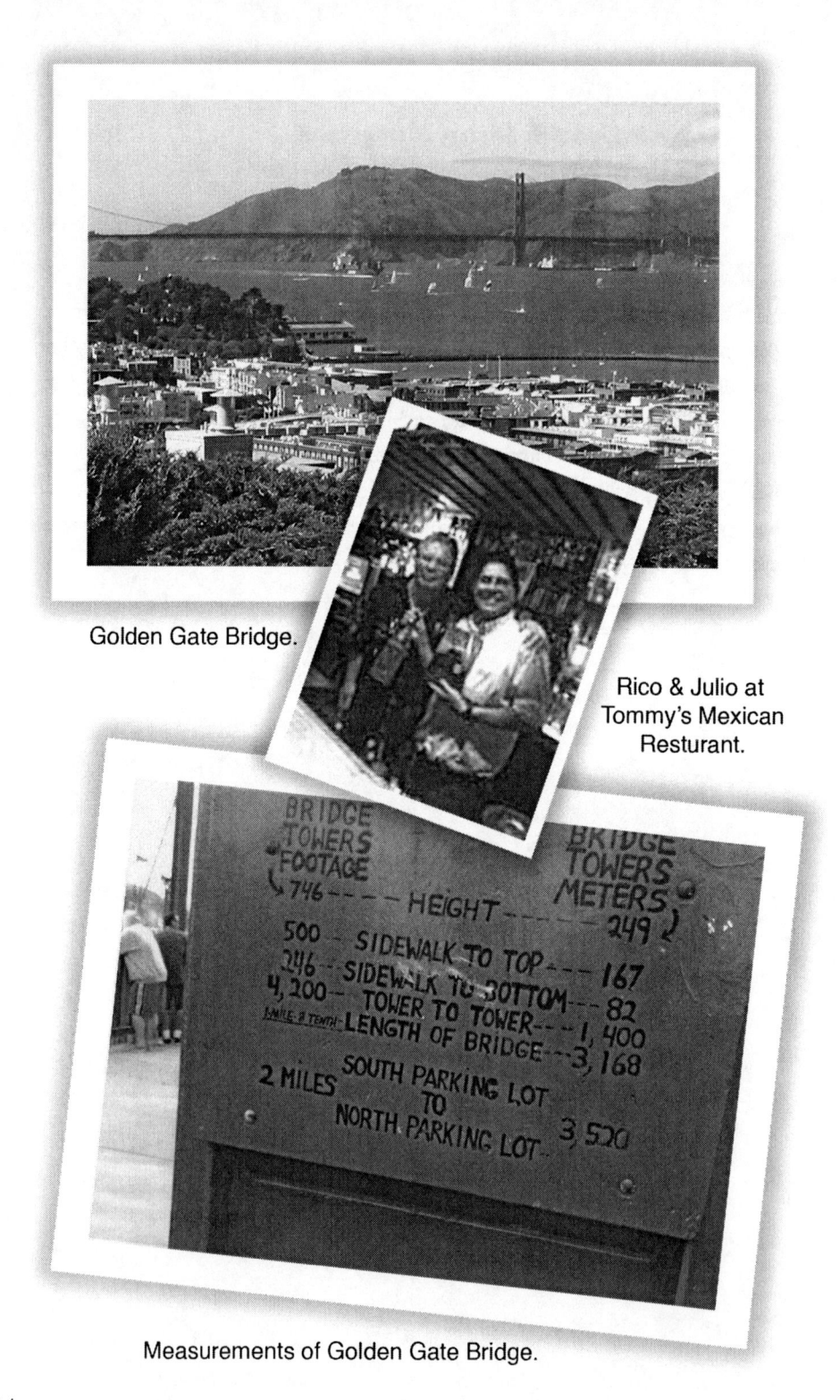

Golden Gate Bridge.

Rico & Julio at Tommy's Mexican Resturant.

Measurements of Golden Gate Bridge.

On Golden Gate Bridge, Alcatraz Island in the distance.

115

Marin County side of the Golden Gate Bridge.

116

John Dennis Smith aka John Starr.

John Dennis Smith & his band, notice the ELVIS coozie cup.

John Dennis Smith with his band, "Southern Thunder," playing music at "The Running of the Bulls" in Cave Creek Arizona.

Chapter 9
The No Good, the Bad and the Ugly

October 24th, 2012

I wonder, "Why I quit gambling, why I gave up Blackjack, the game of 21 that consumed most of my time and my thoughts." I pondered this heavily as I left the office of my personal doctor, Dr. Robert Rauscher Jr. MD, late that October morning.

It was one week before Halloween; United Nations Day and I could not have been in a worse nightmare had Count Dracula personally sunk his fangs into my sun drenched neck.

If I would have continued gambling, most likely I would not have been leaving the doctor's office frightened of an early, of an untimely death. When I had begun the healing process of my compulsive sickness that relied on playing black jack and betting on football games, I had started to write again. Writing words had taken the place of counting cards.

Who would have known or even guessed that writing novels would outrank hanging out in casinos on the danger scale. Here I was, in the zone of perilous endings, for no other reason than having written a story about things that happened in my life of younger years that included tequila and a spring break trip gone awry.

October 24, 2012;

I leave Dr. Rauscher's office with a prescription of AMOX – CLAV 500 MG Tablets, qty 20; There are only 2 other people waiting at the Walgreen's counter located just off Dynamite Road. I wait for only about three minutes and I'm called to the counter, I hand the female attendant, (she was not the pharmacist) the scribbled almost impossible to read prescription form and she tells me that my order will be ready in approximately two hours. I thank her and return home.

Three hours later I return to Walgreen's and am handed a prescription bottle with 20 of the tablets and the Pharmacist consults with me that I am to take 2 tablets per day for ten days continuously. I thank him and return home with the stapled sack.

INGREDIENT NAME: AMOXICILLIN (a-MOX-i-SIL-in) and CLAVULANATE (KLAV-ue-la-nate) COMMON USES: This medicine is a penicillin antibiotic used to treat infections caused by certain bacteria. BEFORE USING THIS MEDICINE: Some medicines or medical conditions may interact with this medicine. INFORM YOUR DOCTOR OR PHARMACIST of all prescription and over-the-counter medicine that you are taking. DO NOT ………. HOW TO USE THIS MEDICINE: Follow the directions for taking this medicine provided by your doctor. Take this medicine by mouth at the start of a meal …….. CAUTIONS: DO NOT TAKE THIS MEDICINE if you have had an allegoric reaction to it, to any ingredient in this product, or to another penicillin antibiotic … POSSIBLE SIDE EFFECTS: SIDE EFFECTS that my occur while taking this medicine include diarrhea, nausea, or vomiting. If they continue or are ………….. OVERDOSE: IF OVERDOSE IS SUSPECTED, contact your local poison control center or emergency room immediately. Symptoms may include decreased ……… ADDITIONAL INFORMATION: If your symptoms do not improve or if they become worse, contact your doctor. DO NOT SHARE THIS MEDICINE with ….

This is the first time that I had ever read through its entirety, the directions, the smaller print after the small print of any prescription because of how bad the lesion on my arm looked, the joint area where blood is normally taken from your vein when you give blood, plasma or are getting blood work done as was I.

This message goes out to the sick fuck that stuck me with the needle and to all the other sick fucks including terrorists and to those scattered throughout this world that do harm to innocent victims and children: You can not and will not break the goodness of the human spirit and the love of living free, to practice our chosen religion, to live life with happiness and hope. Here is to freedom!! You are outnumbered by the goodness and will not conquer.

And a personal note to the warped individual: Yes, I did suffer on the toilet from the antibiotic; but, it was nothing compared to the suffering of my mind, wondering if …….. while awaiting the results this initial time, in three months and then again in six months. Still, I cherish life each day and continue to smile. I pray that GOD will protect me and heal me and that perhaps you will throw down your evil ways and rise up as a contributing citizen of society.

I write to warn others of the dangers that lurk our neighborhoods, our streets and our cities so that they be might be aware that there are disgusting misfits among us that choose to do us harm because of their unhappiness, whether chosen or not. If they be so miserable, then why not end their own selfish, unproductive lives and leave ours to prosper and grow.

October 24th, 2012; 8:20 pm;
The home phone rings, I contemplate not answering, because it is most likely a telemarketer telling me I've won a free trip and now all I need to do is give them a credit card number for a different trip before the actual trip of which I was drawn as the grand prize winner. I listened to three more rings and saved my last few lines of writing before answering. "Hello, yes this is Rico."

"Hi, Dr. Rauscher, thank you very much for taking the time to call me." Yes, that is good news. So the x rays came up negative of any foreign object in my arm near the elbow area. Fantastic, thanks again and have a good rest of the evening," and I hung up the phone with a just a bit of relief. I then shared the news with Connie.

"When do they think they'll have the blood results?" she asked.

"Dr. Rauscher told me possibly by this coming Friday, I do hope so. I don't want to have to wonder about it over the weekend. At least I should know before I head out to Las Vegas for the SEMA Show next Tuesday morning."

October 26th, 2012; around 4:00 pm

"Hello, this is Rico Austin calling to find out if the results from my blood work has been brought back to your office."

"Hold on while I check, sorry nothing yet. Try checking again with us early next week," came the reply of Stephanie's caring voice on the other end of the line.

"Oh, okay, I'll try back on Monday, thanks." I hung up the phone and hung my head. I'm worried, scared and agitated. With nothing else in the way of alternatives to get through this other than faith, I take the time to thank GOD for all his blessings and ask for a favor in the way of prayer, that HE the Almighty, please heal me of all sickness, give my mind strength and that these recent tests would come back in the negative form.

October 29th, 2012; late afternoon

"Yes, this is he; Thank goodness. Yes, I'll be sure to come in to see Dr. Rauscher in three months for another round of blood tests. So all these tests came back negative, right? Great, thank you, thank you." As I put the receiver back on its hook, I began to cry tears of relief, tears of thankfulness and tears of forgiveness. "Thank YOU Dear GOD," I whispered towards the heavens. I was no longer dreading my work week in Las Vegas, standing on the convention floor in our company booth, demonstrating new products, visiting with customers and prospecting for new clientele. I was ecstatic of being alive, of being free of a horrible disease or virus, at least for the time being. I was back to normal for another twelve weeks. I picked up the phone again, this time to tell Connie of the blessing news.

October 31st, 2012;

I've been in Vegas now for two days and tonight is Halloween. All I can say is, WoW! You can't tell the professionals from the amateurs, (I'm talking about hookers, women of the night, prostitutes). A fair share of the girls and women have most of their skin showing, no matter how cool the night air is. There were a couple of gals at Treasure Island that were escorted to the front door due to their costume or may we say because of lack of clothing material.

November 2nd, 2012; 5:30 pm;

"This is where you can set up your books, signage and whatever else you have," Michael the manager of Diablo's guided me to an open table in the side section of his restaurant. "Anything you need, just ask one of the bartenders and if they can't accommodate you, then have them get me. I'll be in the office or upstairs. Thanks for coming in and doing this book signing. Rico, what would you like to drink?"

"I'll take a blended margarita with salt, please. Thank you for having me and the invitation. Here, I have an autographed copy of "My Bad Tequila" for you. I do hope you enjoy it and "Have a Double Shot of Reality," I added my trademark phrase for more emphasis and fun.

"Oh, I didn't ask you, how was the SEMA show this week?" Michael asked as he smoothed his short beard and mustache.

"It was pretty darn busy. I would say a bit better than last year, it was a good show, were you able to make it over for a visit?"

"No, unfortunately or fortunately, this place has me hopping all the time. We've been running this band play off for the last couple of months upstairs in the night club, but we're finally down to the last two bands," Michael shared with me. "We'll talk later, good luck and sell a shitload of books."

My amigo Les G. from Denver came in later that night, we had worked together at Michelin North America back in the late 1990s and early 2000s. Les and his wife Molly were good friends of both Connie and I, they had even come down to San Carlos, Mexico with us during Labor Day weekend in 2009. The two of them had flown in from Denver and we had picked them up at Sky Harbor International Airport and the four of us had tried to drive down to our condo. We eventually made it 36 hours later, due to the worst hurricane to hit landfall at Guaymas or San Carlos in tens of years. They had been good sports about it, even though we had to stay one night in Hermosillo and there was no power for the first day of our arrival. Les and Molly did get to use their diving gear and they were impressed with the visibility even with the water having been churned up during the storm.

"This is a pretty cool restaurant here at the Monte Carlo, how have book sales been tonight?" Les asked.

"Yeah, I like it here. You need to try their margaritas and I sold a few books at the bar and to some of the folk having dinner in the restaurant. If I see Michael, the manager of this place, I'll introduce you, and then I'm ready to go party," I strongly suggested.

November 3rd, 2012;

I'm speeding down the highway, headed for home with head throbbing and radio blasting. It was a good week and I'm thankful to be living this life.

November 2012;

Have you ever heard the saying, "Too many cooks in the kitchen?" Or "Too many cooks spoil the broth?" Yes, I was sure that most of you had heard one or both of these phrases and the next couple of pages will give you a great example of the meaning.

From: Rico Austin
Subject: Hello Rich
To: Rich Carl….
Date: Tuesday, November 13, 2012, 7:18 pm
Hello Rich, John asked me to send You an email introducing myself. Gracias & Best Regards, rico
"Have a Double Shot of Reality" TM
Rico Austin Author - "My Bad Tequila"

Hollywood Book Festival - Honorable Mention (Wild Card genre 2011)
Readers Favorite Book Awards - Silver (Fiction - Mystery - General genre 2011)
Amazon eKindle - #1 Top Rated Kindle eBooks (Mexico Travel genre 2011)
"Five Parrots in a Palm Tree" - Superb Island Reading Award 2011
#1 Book to Read, June 2011 - NY Professional Reviewer, Fran Lewis
Readers' Favorite Book Awards - Finalist (Fiction - General genre 2011)
Arizona Authors Association - 3rd Place (Fiction Book of the Year 2011 - 2012)

London Book Festival - Honorable Mention (Wild Card genre 2012)

New Mexico – Arizona Book Awards – Finalist (Fiction – Mystery genre 2012)

Los Angeles Book Festival - Honorable Mention (Wild Card genre 2011-2012)

New York Beach Book Festival - Honorable Mention (General Non-Fiction genre 2012)

Bibliocracy.com - Author of the Month (June 2012)

Suspense Magazine - Review & Article (July 2012 issue)

Co- Songwriter - "My Bad Tequila"

Songwriter - "Havin' a Beer on the Santa Monica Pier"

http://amazon.com/author/rico.austin   www.mybadtequila.com
Tel: (480) …-…. Cell: (480) ….-… cell
http://blog.mybadtequila.com

Now you may be wondering what all of the other crap aka pertinent marketing material is on the page following the email. Please let me explain: If you should ever receive an email from my personal email address, then you would also receive all this same information as part of my signature. A great long time ago I learned a valuable lesson, "If you don't believe in and promote yourself and your work, then no one else is going to do it for you." And so, I have all the awards and accolades listed along with my website and blog info. But, do not fret as this is the only time that it will be listed as I consider it part of the story and of who I truly am. This is called character development.

From: Rich Carl….
Subject: Hello Rich
To: Rico Austin
Date: Wednesday, November 14, 2012, 9:09 am
Good morning Rico. I have been looking forward to meeting you, and discussing the book project. Is there a good time to meet together? Thanks, Rich

November 14th, 2012; 4:00 pm
I pull into the Starbucks in a shopping center just off to the right of North Scottsdale Road and see John and this other guy in a chair next to

him that obviously, must be his friend Rich. They are sitting at an outside table in front of the Seattle based coffee shop.

A bit apprehensive, I walk slower than usual to the round table with an umbrella fully extended giving plenty of shade on this brisk day.

They both wave to me, making sure I see them. I wave back and manage a smile.

After all the introductions were made and some small talk about the weather, we got down to business with Rich Carl…. starting the conversation. "As you probably now know, I am spearheading this book project and I have been in touch with a publisher since we are no longer working with Jane Dystel. The name of the publisher is 'Tate Publishing' based out of Oklahoma and for $3800 they will publish and market the book for us."

I interrupted, "What happened to the $1.5 million offer from Dystel and Goderich?" This is hard for me to get my head around it, at first we were going to receive money for writing 'Let the Boy Sing, Elvis was My Daddy,' and now we're paying a publisher $3800. "What happened?" I looked at John and then at Rich Carl…. for an explanation.

"I guess they lied," John volunteered an answer.

"Who lied?" I asked.

"Jane Dystel and her company," said John.

"Okay, anything else that I need to hear?" I pressed onward.

"Well, Rich said that if you and he both write the book together we can have it done in a less than a month, and to the publisher."

"Where is the $3800 coming from?" I pushed.

"I was thinking we could sell shares or percentages of the book to investors and raise the money," Rich answered as if this was a great idea.

"You're kidding right? This is a book we're talking about, not a piece of land," I shook my head in disbelief at what I had just heard and for a mere $3800.

"Have you any better ideas," Rich challenged.

"How about we just split the costs, if this is the way we need to go," I offered my opinion. "In fact I can probably come up with half of it, but, I will need to think this over. It is quite a bit for me to digest at this time, between halving the writing of the novel between Rich and I and having to pay to get this thing off the ground."

"Yeah, that's a good idea, Rico. Think it over and let me know what you think you'd like to do," said John, trying to sound as upbeat as possible.

"I'm heading out to Miami tomorrow to accept my 2011 Readers' Favorite Award for "My Bad Tequila" and to have a book signing while out there, so I'll think it over and let you know when I return next week," I said as I slowly rose from my seat.

November 15th, 2012; 3:24 pm

Pulling my suitcase and with my laptop hanging from my right shoulder, I make my way to the shuttle kiosk outside the Miami airport and ask for the fare to the downtown Hilton.

November 15th, 2012; 7:10 pm

The taxi drops me off in front of the Hyatt Regency in downtown Miami and I walk to the front desk and ask for directions to the conference room where the 'Readers Favorite' happy hour is being hosted.

A pleasant, short, grayish haired Hispanic woman looks at her directory and apologizes as she does not find any such organization.

"Are you sure?" "Is there another Hyatt Regency in Miami?" I questioned as I checked my phone for the time.

"Si, I mean yes, this is the only Hyatt Regency," she said, trying to be helpful.

I asked if I might use their business center to double check my yahoo email to make sure I was at the right place on the right date.

The patient and polite lady gave me a key card and directed me to the business center where there were five desktop computers available for use by guests.

Quickly I found the invitation and read it again, this time noticing and jotting down the address and hotel which was the Regency Hotel, there was no Hyatt leading the Regency and this place was near the airport. I thanked the lady, gave her back the key card, ran out the door and asked the doorman to please hail me a taxi. He beckoned for one lined up near the parking garage and I was on my way to meet Paul Michael Glaser aka David Starsky of the hit series in the seventies of 'Starsky and Hutch.' Paul had been a selected winner in the children's genre with his new book, 'Chrystallia and the Source of Light.' He was also asked to be a guest speaker at the awards ceremony on Saturday and I had received word from Readers' Favorite CEO and founder, Debra Gaynor that Starsky would be making an appearance at the social mixer aka happy hour. This was the only reason I was spending my first evening at a hotel bar, I wanted to meet David Starsky and give him a limited edition, signed copy of my award winning book. I did meet Starsky and he did ask me to please call him Paul and not Starsky. I was the only one he had to advise of that, everyone else had chosen to call him by his real name, which to me was no fun, but, I obliged and had a pleasant conversation about all the changes we are seeing in this world of ours. We also spoke of the overall sad affairs of Congress, of other politics and of those that are leading our country down a dangerous path of possible destruction.

I did see Paul Michael Glaser again the next day at the Miami Book Fair where he was selling autographed copies of 'Chrystallia' to children and their parents.

Paul saw me walk by and hollered, "Hey Rico, how's it going?"

I took this as an invitation to visit his booth, where he thanked me again for my book given him the night before. He then suggested I buy a copy of his book. I told him I didn't want to carry anything around with me, that I would have him sign me over a copy at the Awards Ceremony the next afternoon. To this, he replied, "These are all the books I have left, so you'd better buy one now before they're completely sold out." I looked at the small stack of fifteen or so copies lying on the table and pulled a twenty dollar bill from my money clip. Paul signed it and I went about my way, checking out publishers, authors, literary agents, publicists and food vendors. After a couple of hours I ended back near Paul Michael Glaser's booth and to my astonishment and dismay, he had dozens and dozens of copies of his novel placed on the long, retractable table.

"What? Starsky had looked me in the eye and lied to me, telling me he was nearly out of copies, thus giving the perception of scarcity which in turn sped up my buying process," I calculated the event in my mind. "Was this an all out blatant lie or a well rehearsed sales technique that had worked?" as I questioned this in my mind, I did come to the conclusion that 1975 Gran Torinos painted reddish orange were no longer one of my favorite movie muscle cars.

South Beach was beckoning for a visit from its dear ol' amigo, Rico, as I hadn't stepped foot in that white soft sand since the early part of 2000. The music and memory of over twelve years earlier guided me into Mango's Tropical Cafe at 900 Ocean Drive to watch the flamenco dancers. A couple of nice hours of sipping margaritas and chatting with tourists had the evening going well. That was until I'd met an immaculately dressed, over weight Hispanic man with perfect polished, manicured nails who I guessed to be about thirty five years old. This guy claimed to be the son of a retired drug dealer from Columbia and begged for me to become his ghostwriter and together we would make millions. Javier had pestered me non-stop after seeing me hand the bartender one of my book markers. I carry around plenty of book markers and hand out them out freely in lieu of business cards to help promote my book and it's a great icebreaker.

When giving it to a bartender, it sometimes sparks a fire and the bartender tries to impress me with the best flavored margarita that I've ever tasted, since my book marker touts me not only as a writer but also a Tequila Connoisseur. I wanted to get away from Javier and his never ending cocaine stories. Some of his tales had him as buying, while others had him selling. Some of his stories included shootouts similar, all too similar, to the one played out by Al Pacino in 'Scarface.' Only difference is, Javier and his dad don't die, they never get shot and they always get the chicas. His constant interruptions with a Columbian South Beach accent broke my concentration of trying intently to gape at the curves and exposed skin of the female dancing artists. And his hands, his perfectly manicured hands looked as if never had they gripped a gun nor pistol whipped a single bad soul. Finally, unable to allow my ears to listen to even one more bloody scenario of drug deals gone bad, I excused myself to the bathroom and headed out the front door via a long trip around the bar to explore a new locale.

"Hey Rico, where you heading out to?" I heard a non Columbian and definitely not a South Beach accent questioning me. I turned to see Tom, the husband of fellow Author, Kelly Lee. I had met Tom and his wife Kelly at the social function at the Regency. He had recognized me as I was bolting from the Mango. Kelly had won the Readers' Favorite Gold award in her genre for "Murdering Eve," her first novel.

"Not really sure, just need a change of scenery. I've been here a while so just moving up the road, how about you?" I replied and questioned back. Kelly then came into view as did a couple of her girl friends from Dallas who'd come out to share in the awards ceremony and, to tie in a long weekend getaway in Florida.

"Why don't you go with us to LIV, the famous night club at Fontainebleau?" asked Tom.

"Do you know what, that sounds like a great idea," and I followed them to the car, we drove to and entered one of the most extravagant clubs in Florida. It was a great time, except for the extreme, ridiculous pricing of cocktails and beer. My one and only visit to this hotspot. Too hot for my wallet.

November 17th, 2012; late afternoon

At the awards ceremony being held at the Regency Hotel, Paul Michael Glaser asked me to pose with him for a picture, both of us holding our winning novels. I once again dig 1975 Gran Torinos, no matter what the color.

I had the pleasure to meet with and share in delightful conversation with another award winning author, who had a British accent. "I saw from your biography that you attended school at Staffordshire in Stoke-on-Trent, England," and then he announced himself as Lonnie Beerman.

I kindly asked for the name of his award winning novel and he replied, "'Tears of the Phoenix,' which explores complex human relationships by chronicling the adventures, heartbreaks and triumphs of three young boys and their families in a small southern town during the socially tumultuous 1960's."

"Sounds interesting," I complemented as I knew it must be good or else he wouldn't have been in Miami collecting a gold medal for his story.

He then introduced me to his wife, (her name escapes me) and told me that she had studied and received her degree at Arizona State University as he noticed from my biography that I resided in the Scottsdale area.

I then made the comment about having "Phoenix" in the title and Lonnie told me that it was just coincidental. I found out they now lived in the New England area. We talked about it being strange that we both had lived in Stoke-on-Trent and had both lived in the Phoenix area. Lonnie asked me if I was working on a new book or story and I replied, "Yes, I'm doing an interesting autobiography of Elvis' legitimate, illegitimate son who lives just down the road from me in sunny Arizona."

"Fascinating!" was his first word and his face immediately lit with brilliance. "I've got an Elvis story for you," he excitedly continued, and I listened carefully to each word.

"Many years ago, when I lived in Stoke, the council people in and around Stoke-on-Trent had a meeting and determined that we would invite Elvis Presley to come and perform for us, as they all knew it would not be a problem to sell out as many tickets as needed to pay for the show. An amount of $5 million was offered for Elvis to come to England to sing for us and this is the response we received from Tom Parker, better known as "The Colonel," Elvis' manager. "That amount will take care of my part, now what about Elvis?" was the smug reply to a country of Englishmen who were huge Elvis fans. This was a kick to the teeth of every citizen of the United Kingdom is what I gathered from the story.

I questioned Mr. Beerman for more of an explanation, claiming extreme ridiculousism on the part of the The Colonel. Lonnie Beerman agreed with my evaluation and continued with his understanding of why Elvis's manager had made such a farfetched and unfair counter offer. Lonnie had given me a different perspective of who Tom Parker was, after, his full story was told. It began something like this: "He was born Andreas Cornelis van Kuijk in Breda, the Netherlands and was an illegal alien in the United States, he refused to leave for fear of not being able to get back into the country that had helped make him a multi millionaire because of lack of having a passport. Also there were questions about a murder in Breda in which Van Kuijk, (as he was known) aka Parker might have been a suspect or at least a person of interest. This is most likely the reason that Parker never applied for a passport after arriving illegally in the U.S. when he was just 17 years of age as he could have been extradited back to his Dutch beginnings. Tom Parker never left the country nor did he allow Elvis to perform outside the U.S. except when Elvis was serving overseas in the armed forces."

"Wow, I'm flabbergasted, I had no fricking idea," I exclaimed while shaking my head in disbelief.

"Yes, Elvis, his songs and his memory are still huge in England, in fact when you have your book finished, please get in touch with me because my family absolutely adores Elvis. They would love to read this story," he finished.

"Lonnie, I'll tell this right now, I will commit to having a book signing in the Stoke-on-Trent area when this is published. In fact, we'll try to arrange a concert with John Dennis Smith if he agrees and it will be much less than $5 million," I promised my new author friend.

"That would be great, in fact, I would bet that just with my relatives alone we'd sell 100 seats and 100 books," was the forecast of his family participation made by Lonnie.

"Stoke never got their concert with Elvis, but, they will have Elvis' son belting out hits by his Daddy, for you and your countrymen," I proclaimed proudly as I knew this would be making a wish come true for many of the United Kingdom. I know that they do love their pints, their football and their music. And, I had just learned that they still love Elvis Presley.

Later that evening I had a book signing at the oldest bar in Miami, 'Tobacco Road' which was celebrating its 100th year birthday on November 16th, 2012. I was honored to be included in the festivities. I sold fifteen books and gave away another six for a grand total of twenty one new readers, one of whom was an entrant and finalist in the extreme moustache contest.

> From: Rich Carl….
> Subject: John Smith
> To: Rico Austin
> Date: Wednesday, November 21, 2012, 3:44 pm
> Hi Rico,
>
> I spoke with John, and he indicated that you are still working on the book, but from your messaging last night, that you were stepping back from your involvement in the writing, and wished him good luck. That is fine if you wish to be free of the burden of the book. I did want to clarify a few things from my perspective. When we left our last meeting, you were going to think about things for a few days, and we would talk when you returned from Florida. Some more things have changed, so please do not write anything more until we talk. That is, if you still want to be part of the process. Regardless of what John has told you, I am in charge of the book process. It is through my efforts and my writings, that representation, and contracts, have been obtained. John gets great ideas of trying to do things on his own, or his own way. He is also big hearted without thinking things through, and this can lead to confusion and misunderstandings. You

are not the first one to be a party to this. Some of it is also attributed to the everchanging (sic) nature of the entertainment business. All this being said, if your proposal was acceptable to Jane, the original plan could still be moving forward. Because that did not happen, we are moving in another direction. If you would like to discuss this further, please let me know. If you have had enough of this venture, that is fine also.

Thank you for your time, and I await your response.

Thanks, Rich Carl....

From: Rico Austin
Subject: Re: John Smith
To: Rich Carl....
Date: Wednesday, November 21, 2012, 5:02 pm

Hi Rich, I am thoroughly confused as to what is going on. I am writing a book, recieved (sic) information from John and never withdrew from the project, wrote to him that I would not be "in" tomorrow meaning at home, as I would be visiting customrs (sic) as he said he would call in the morning. I did write that communication has been poor and that we need to change that. I did wish him to get better and good luck. I initially had to wait for Karen Albright Lin to be cleared off project, and John & Lisas (sic) told me I was their author and now another new change as John tells me that he has another guy named Rich involved and sent me your email address last week. I then was told last week also that Karen has filed a lawsuit as she feels she was led down a wrongful path. John called me this morning and told me that he now has a job and that was why he couldn't talk yesterday. I told him that I believe I can come up with the $3800; $2000 on my credit card and borrow from a friend in Idaho the $1800 and he says great, now talk with Rich. I don't want to be financially supporting this whole thing and then be told that another person is in charge. Something seems very amiss here. I wrote a successful novel already on my own and I can do another. When too many people get involved nothing happens or if it does, everyone loses. I was very excited about the project and have been involved since July 14th and have written over 70 pages; Gracias & Best Regards, rico

From: Rich Carl....
Subject: John Smith
To: Rico Austin
Date: Thursday, November 21, 2012, 5:17 pm
Hi Rico,

I can understand the confusion. This project is my idea, and I have been making it happen since its' inception, in April. From the time that you were first mentioned to me, I have been asking John to meet you, and if you know about me, and what my role is. That apparently did not happen. Regardless, that is the situation. If you would like to meet and discuss this, I will make myself available. I have a copy of a text message indicating that you "don't think I'm in, too many changes, and never able to communicate..."

From: Rico Austin
Subject: Re: John Smith
To: Rich Carl....
Date: Wednesday, November 21, 2012, 5:27 pm
Hi Rich,

Thanks for agreeing that there is / has been confusion. As you know from our meeting last week that I was told that there was an offer of 1.5 million on the table of which I would receive 50% less 15% off the top. Then I found out that this was not so and still have not received a good answer other than "they lied," meaning the literary agent and her company. Are you John's manager? He had always told me that his manager was H.T. I would like to know the whole story before making a decision to go on my own with writing the biography.

Gracias & Best Regards, rico

From: Rico Austin
Subject: Re: John Smith
To: Rich Carl....
Date: Wednesday, November 22, 2012, 11:25 am

Hi Rich, Gracias for the email and invite; as per your text below: "Hi Rico, I was having a family dinner, and was not available. If you have some time on Friday, I will make myself available to meet with you. How about the Starbucks where we met last time. Let me know a time that works (sic) you."

Rich, Yes, a meeting on Friday would be great. How about 10:00 am at Pima and Pinnacle Peak; it is on the west side of Pima, there is a little store there with post office inside as I need to mail some books. Gracias & Best Regards, Rico

From: Rich Carl….
Subject: John Smith
To: Rico Austin
Date: Thursday, November 22, 2012, 9:07 pm
I will see you at ten at the general store.

November 23th, 2012; 10:06 am
I hurriedly exited the car and entered through the stone archway that leads into the courtyard and then to the General Store and other specialty shops such as art galleries and antique shops. I had grabbed the brass handle of the door and was pulling it open when Rich Carl…. spoke and caught my attention. "I'm over here," he spoke while seated on the wooden bench.

I moved toward him and thrust my hand out as a peace offering, "Hi, sorry I'm a bit late, I was busy writing and the time escaped me," I apologized.

"No problem," he said as he noisily shuffled the file of papers he had with him. "Why don't we sit here," as he went to the picnic bench under the canopy.

"Hey, Rich I didn't mention this to you when I met you for the first time at the Star Bucks with John Smith. You look almost exactly like my friend Jonathon that used to live here in Cave Creek, but has moved out to Buckeye, southwest of here."

"Yeah, I've been told several times that I look exactly like another guy around these parts. In fact, once I almost got into a fight with a gal at a restaurant because she says, 'Hey, you're already back,' and I tell her I've never been in that place before and she tells me, 'you were just here yesterday,' and I told her that I would know if I were here yesterday and the conversation just continued to get worse."

I sat across from him and let him begin the book conversation.

"I want you to know that I am in charge of this project and John has given me full responsibility of all writing. He will do the music end and I the book," he stated, in a self satisfying way.

"Well, I've written quite a bit, spent a great deal of time on this; however, I am willing to co-author this with you to get it finished," I offered a truce.

"I don't think that is now possible," he grinned slightly while saying these words to me.

"Why not? I thought that is what John wanted, for us to get this done and work together," I stated with puzzled anxiety.

"Well, for beginners, you have plagiarized me," he accused.

"Say what?" I questioned in disbelief. My face reddened, my heart quickened and my blood heated at this accusation. There is not a worse word to be associated with a writer, an author than plagiarism. It is one of the worst things that anyone can possibly associate you with. I was pissed and ready for a brawl.

"Yes, the one piece about the note written on the back of the frame, you know about 'Let the Boy Sing.'" Once again, I glared in disbelief at this weirdo guy named Rich that was nothing like my true and best friend Rich in Idaho and who was nothing like my buddy Jonathon. This bad Rich only shared the same name with one and looked physically alike as my other friend, Jonathon; yet, he was not a good person as were the other two.

"Rich, you're crazy, John told me the exact wording and I read it on the sheet itself, although it was hard to read," I defended myself.

"Well, it must have been divine intervention then, because that is the exact phrase, if you didn't plagiarize," he boasted.

"Rich, that is the worst thing you could have said to me as I take pride in my writing and you know I did not plagiarize you," I stood my ground. I wanted in the worst way to come across that table and kick his smug ass about twelve different ways from tomorrow. I'd make it a baker's dozen, yeah one more, an odd thirteen was what this prick deserved. "No, this is a public place and too many witnesses," I reasoned to myself. "I don't need to see the inside of Sheriff Joe Arpaio's jail cell or tent city because of this ass wipe and his outrageous and false accusations."

"Well, that is the way it is and I am not going to have you on the project," he continued, "and besides your writing style does not fit well for this book."

Now, my blood was near 212 degrees Fahrenheit, ready to boil any second, "Listen, I don't know who you think you are, coming in here like you're an attorney or something with your file of paper, but Lisa and John and a bunch of other people all loved my novel "My Bad Tequila" and that is the reason I am here." I finished with, "And how many books or published articles have you written?" knowing good and well he couldn't write any better than an eighth grader doing a homework report on the subject of "Why people think I'm a flaming asshole."

"Was Lisa drinking when she read your book?" he snarled with an evil grin. Then he added, "John doesn't know what he is saying half the time as he is trying to please everyone. That is why I'm in charge of this whole thing," he insulted.

I lost my cool, stood up and said, "You're not a friend to John or Lisa, a true friend would not say anything like you've told a stranger such as me. I'm in agreement that I can not work with you, I don't want to work with an unethical, backstabbing person like yourself. I will write my own book and it will be read, it will be sold and I will be proud of it. In the end you'll have nothing, surely not friends," I angrily orated and turned my back on a human filled with poisonous venom. I wheeled around and faced him once more exasperated as I added, "I plan on telling John and Lisa exactly what you think of them," and turned my back forever on Sodom and Gomorrah.

"Hey, you're free to write whatever you want, but you're not going to write "Let the Boy Sing," he shouted after me. I just continued to walk with my back to the disgusting, miserable being.

I called Connie on my way home and told her of the treacherous meeting and the vile words that spewed from Rich Carl....'s mouth. I pledged to let John and Lisa know the thoughts and words of the underhanded guy they were in bed with and of whom I would not lie between the covers next to, nor be associated in any form or way.

After getting home and cooling off a bit, I dialed John's cell and when he answered I said, "The meeting did not go well. I just want to let you know that there are no hard feelings, I'm not involved in the project; however, I would like to talk with you if I can stop by this afternoon."

"Yeah, sure, please come by, I just got off the phone with Rich and he told me, "I got rid of Rico," and I told him, "You were suppose to work together, not to end it with him."

John then asked me, "Rico, please reconsider, we need to talk."

"I'll be over in about half an hour," and hit the red, end button on the phone.

It was the day after Thanksgiving, Connie and I had roasted a turkey and had put together a full smorgasbord of mashed potatoes, turkey stuffing, corn, sweet potatoes, olives, gravy and bread. We had lots of leftovers since it was just her and I at the table so I gathered some turkey, some potatoes and gravy, wrapped it up in foil over a paper plate and took it to Cave Creek with me to show that there was no animosity and that our relationship would remain positive and good. I knocked on the door and heard the familiar, "C'mon in,"

"What's it you got there amigo?" John questioned.

"Oh, just some turkey and potatoes, we had so much left over and I didn't know if you guys had turkey or not, so here you are," I handed him the plate and he placed it in the refrigerator.

"Thanks, you didn't need to do that."

"I know, just had lots of turkey and I wanted to let you and Lisa know that I am disappointed I won't be working on your story; but, there is no way in hell that I will have anything to do with Rich," I finished speaking as Lisa entered the kitchen. "Hi Lisa," I gave her a hug and then told them word for word as best as I could about the encounter with Rich and warned them that he was not a friend.

Lisa then said, "This is not the first time that we've heard this about Rich," then looked at John and continued, "You need to have a talk with him, this shit needs to stop."

John added, "Rico, don't make a final decision just yet, I'll speak with Rich and we'll figure this out."

To which I replied, "John, there is no way I am going to work with Rich as I find him to be very shady, corrupt and condescending. He is not a nice person and as long as he is involved, I will not be. But, this in no way should affect our friendship. Okay, now come here and give me a big hug."

*Note to Readers, AuthorHouse is the publishing company of which I agreed to have my first Children's book, "ARIZONA Is Where I Live" published. The emails below are between Rico Austin, the Author and Cindy Work, the Illustrator.

From: Rico Austin
Subject: Author House – ARIZONA is Where I Live
To: Cindy Work
Date: Tuesday, November 27, 2012, 4:10 pm
Hello Amiga,

I paid the $ by cc for the Voyager Package, click onto link below to see; Whenever You get a chance, just put a check in the mail for $... and a copy of that will be your receipt for tax write off if you decide to claim it as a business to offset taxes on future sales!

http://www.authorhouse.com/servicesstore/choosechildrens.asp
make check out to: Rico Austin

Also, please talk to Connie about coming in and doing the scanning of artwork when ready. I'll have the last week of December off to help send things in, etc.

How close are you to finishing? We're almost there! Yee Haw & Congrats on a Great Job!

Gracias & Best Regards, Rico

From: Cindy Work
Subject: Re: Author House – ARIZONA is Where I Live
To: Rico Austin
Date: Tuesday, November 27, 2012, 7:26 pm

Ok very good! I will get check to you. I did want Jim to talk to you about the publishing. I don't think I retained all that you told me. When is a good time to talk to Con, weekends? And yes I have 1 more to draw, the capital building. Plus the faces of the sweaty kids. Hope to work on them this week. It has been hectic!

Tell her to call me when it is convenient for her. Talk to you soon.
Cindy

December 6th, 2012;

I received a phone call from Amigo Emilio aka Blu Kaboy aka VooDoo Daddy. This is the happening dude that has the strongest

139

connections to getting Boise State football tickets, front row to every home game and away game. He is a season ticket holder, a Boise State degree holder and has worn the most outrageous pimp daddy costumes in the last few years at each and every home game. He travels with one of his three outfits to most away games. "Hey Compadre, are you planning on going to the Maaco Bowl in Las Vegas?"

"Yes, I'm driving over on that Thursday or Friday before. You going?" I asked enthusiastically.

"Absolutely! I'm coming over on a chartered bus from Boise to Vegas. Have you bought your tickets yet?" Before I could respond, Emilio added, "I can get you a ticket in the front row and possibly a couple others if need be."

"I'm there dude! I know my buddy Rich Collins is going, he already has his flight booked on Southwest and we were going to buy our tickets before the game, so go ahead and grab two, por favor."

"One more thing, do you want to wear the Blue Elvis costume? I can bring it with me, I'll get it from my buddy, Johnny V., who lives here in Boise," added Emilio.

"Thank You, thank you very much," I playfully responded. "Is there any way you can get a second for Collins? I think I can talk him into it," I used Rich's last name since Emilio knew who I was talking about.

"I'll find out; but, I will have one for sure, Elvis."

"Great, looking forward to it. Let me know how much we owe you for the tickets. Adios." I hung up the phone and smiled quite completely. The growing pain and agony of not knowing if this might be the last bowl game I went to was put aside briefly, thinking of all the fun possibilities of being a Blue Elvis for a night or two in Vegas, of all places. Of course this experience would have to be recorded and added in the book.

December 7th, 2012; 1:07 pm
Text from VooDoo Daddy: "I got 2 tickets, on front row w me, Waiting to hear back on blue Elvis suits"

December 7th; 2012;
Reply text from me to VooDoo: "Yes, we will wear. Pls bring. Gracias Amigo"

Paul Michael Glaser (Starsky) & Rico Austin accepting their Readers' Favorite Award in Miami.

Rico with fellow Author Kelly Lee, her husband Tom & other Amigas at LIV Nightclub, in Miami Beach.

Chapter 10
Reunited (and it feels so good)

December 17th, 2012; 2:25 pm
Text from John D. Smith: "Hey u in town"

December 17th, 2012; 2:26 pm
"Yes Amigo, what's going on?" I texted back and then decided to dial his number and talk rather than text back and forth all afternoon.

December 17th, 2012; 2:27 pm
I called John and asked, "What's up Amigo?"
"We need to talk, Catch 22, bring a couple of books, I'll pay for them and I'm buying drinks at the bar."
I hesitate, then say, "I'll bring a couple of books; Am I still in?"
"We need to talk about it, it's all good," assured John.
I'll leave here around 3:30 pm as I'm waiting for Connie to come home as we have some personal business to tend. I'm ready to party. I'm on vacation, be there in just a couple of hours, adios."

Texts sent from John Smith to Rico Austin and vice versa:
December 17th, 2012; 3:29 pm "Come on when ur reafyy (sic)" JS

December 17th, 2012; 3:29 pm "Ready" JS

December 17th, 2012; 3:30 pm "Heading there now" RA

143

December 17th, 2012; 3:31 pm "Ok" JS

December 17th, 2012: 3:45 pm "Tap House (sic)" JS

December 17th, 2012; 4:02 pm "Where u at" JS

December 17th, 2012; 4:10 pm "Here" RA

    Hesitantly I walk across the parking lot, enter the Tap Haus and nod my head at the hostess. This fine establishment is right across the street from Harold's which boasts itself as West Heinz Field, that being said, The Tap Haus must then be West Soldier Field, as it hosts Chicago Bear fans. Illinois tourists and transplants from the Windy City fill the Tap Haus on football Sundays, just as does Buffalo Chip Saloon, which shares a parking lot with Harold's. Buffalo Chip serves as Packer territory for the Green Bay fans and serves as a church during the off season. Hard for me to get my head around this one. I don't think I could be sitting on a pew come Sunday morning, being of a spiritual mindset when I had just been in the same place the evening before, (Saturday night) two stepping with full breasted cowgirls wearing low cut tops and tight jeans while downing straight shots of tequila.

    We still need an official Arizona Cardinal hangout in Cave Creek. I think my Amigo, Mr. Mark Bradshaw should dedicate, The Hideaway Grill, located somewhere in Cave Creek, Arizona as, 'Home of the Red Bird.' Bikers enjoy football too!

    I'm filled with excitement, regret, resentment and exhilaration. After all, John had called me. I knew we had a connection with the music thing; we both loved our drink and women; but, there was something more. I shrugged it off as I took off my leather jacket, the last thing that is going to happen tonight is another disappointment. Things were not sitting with me well. I, like the rest of the Western Hemisphere was angry, distraught, confused over the shootings of kindergarten age children in Connecticut. I saw our country slipping, I saw our country at what I hope is at one of its lowest points ever. "What the fuck is going on?" I screamed this several times in my mind, in my head and a couple of times outside my backyard property where only the quail, cotton tail rabbits and coyotes looked up for a brief second at man's insanity.

Just as I had stepped across the threshold of where party life begins and sober life ends, I saw John. He gave me a high five, a man's hug and said, "It's about fucking time you got here, I've got to take a piss. I'm right over there."

I went to where I had thought the finger pointed; I saw a lonesome shot glass that was used, empty and lonely. "That is where John has been," I calculated slowly in my reasoning and grabbed a bar stool.

Swan, yes this is the name of an amigo that doesn't seem to be gay; that is all I have to say. Swan, was at the other end of the bar; I had calculated incorrectly and had wandered much further down the stretch way than necessary. I found this out when John came back from using the boy's room and hollered down at me, "Rico, we're over here." I saw John sitting next to Swan.

John and I talked, chit chat at first and then straight to the "dirt." For those that think this may have a negative cognitive, it does not. What it means to our kinfolk in the South, to git straight after it. No pussy footing around.

John asked, "Are you still in?"

I acted as if I had not heard the question, "Let me show you what I've been doing," as I opened the vanilla envelope to display some of the most artistic drawings I've ever encountered.

"Oh, my gosh, did Connie do these?" John gushed.

"No, her amiga Cindy, a girl she used to work with, has an incredible talent for drawing and illustrations, so we did a joint venture 50 / 50 deal.

"Wow, these pictures are incredible," John proclaimed as he ordered another 'Dirty Margarita' for he and for me.

"Yes, she is quite the talent and do you care to hear the words, the phrases that go, that blend, that bring to life these illustrations to their glorious beginnings and finishes."

John just looked at me and stated, "Read amigo, read."

ARIZONA Is Where I Live

Map of Arizona – page 1

Arizona is nicknamed the Grand Canyon State; the Grand Canyon is over 1 mile deep and is very, very steep. In some places it is 18 miles wide, which is from side to side. (picture of Grand Canyon with Colorado River below, pages 2 & 3)

If by foot the Grand Canyon you did hike or rode a mule, but definitely not a bike… (boy and girl hiking down the Canyon near the bottom with river, pages 4 & 5)

…it would take two days to get back to the top, and you surely would be ready to drink water or a soda pop. (boy and girl each on a mule heading back up the canyon, pages 6 & 7)

In Arizona there are a lot of animals wild and free. How many can you count and how many do you see? (coyote, rattlesnake, javelina, roadrunner, bobcat, scorpion, hawk in desert setting, pages 8 & 9)

My favorite is the Coyote howling at the moon, it sounds like it's singing in own special tune. (coyote howling at full moon in desert, pages 10 & 11)

In Arizona there are several animals and birds to see. Some live on the ground and some live in trees. Some live in holes they did in the ground. In Arizona there are always birds and animals to be found. (deer, quail, rabbit, cardinal, chipmunk, squirrel in mountain setting, pages 12 & 13)

A covey of quail looking for feed. They eat berries, or grass, or sunflower seed. (covey of quail looking for food on the ground with pods and seeds on the ground, pages 14 & 15)

In the summer Arizona is a very warm state. Even at night, when the children play late. (little boy and girl sweating, looking hot wearing shorts and t-shirts, pages 16 & 17)

We go swimming in the summer to stay cool, in our backyard swimming pool. (little boy swimming in a backyard pool, pages 18 & 19)

We sit in the shade of a Palo Verde to read, which by the way, is the Arizona state tree. (little girl sitting under a tree reading a book, pages 20 & 21)

The Saguaro Cactus Bloom is the state flower and the Saguaro Cactus can grow up to 50 feet or taller. It can live to be 200 years old, standing tall, proud and ever so bold. (large saguaro cactus with white and red blooming flowers, pages 22 & 23)

The state capitol building in Phoenix is over 100 years old, and is quite beautiful and scenic with its copper top dome. (city scene with 4 story building or maybe state capitol building in picture, pages 24 & 25)

Woodpeckers and Cactus Wrens eat insects such as beetles. They make nests in the cacti to be protected by the needles. (woodpecker making a home in the cactus and cactus wren nesting in arm of cactus, pages 26 & 27)

In Arizona we have lots of fun things we can do. In the winter there is snow skiing or we ride our Ski-Doos. (boy and girl skiing in the mountains, pages 28 & 29)

Boating and fishing all over the state, makes for a great weekend or vacation date. (boy boating with family and girl fishing, pages 30 & 31)

In the summer I know where I like to go and what I like to do. Do you? (picture of boy swimming in a public pool with lots of other children, pages 32 & 33)

If you live in or just visit our home state, I hope You enjoy ARIZONA. It's Great! (picture of state flag, pages 34 & 35)

Where do you live?
Draw a picture of your state or something fun you like to do. On this page only, please! (open page, page 36)

Where do you live?

Write me a story or poem about your state. On this page only, please! (open page with lines to write on, page 37)

John, mouth agape and intensely, religiously in awe, said, "I love it, and now I'm asking again, will you write my story?"

I responded as I lifted my margarita to my lips that John had purposely purchased for me, "You've known I've always wanted to write your story, from the time I first heard it."

"Well, it's your move amigo."

Again, we shook hands and fifty / fifty was the number configured.

"John, there is something that I need to tell you; time may be of the essence."

After I had filled him in on those details of distraught and the needle, the story that only a night in San Francisco can bring about, of that late afternoon that should not have been; he did not waver, he did not quaver and toasted, "To the book."

I rubbed my finger around the edge of the glass, filtering as much salt as possible, licked the inside of my middle finger and closed my eyes. "Is Rich Car….. aka A. Dick out of the way?"

"Completely, we've decided that you are the one. Everyone that we've talked with seems to love your style of writing and what's most important is that Lisa and I love it. My attorney told me to do what I want to do, not what Rich or anybody else wants me to do. And, for more good news, Karen Lin Albright has sent me a Christmas card and will not be suing me."

I smile, slightly on the outside; however, greatly on the inside. "Yes, you had me amigo, at Hola." We hug. The end; which is now a new beginning! And, I say to myself, "What the fuck am I going to do now? Should I scrap this personal project I've been working on? Should I tell John, 'hey, I've another story that will supersede yours, but….'" Instead, I say, "Hey, I'm going to Vegas on Thursday. Want to hitch a ride? I'm meeting some Idaho amigos for the MAACO Bowl game in Vegas? It'll be an epic trip, I'm going to be dressed as a Blue Elvis.

"What the fuck is a Blue Elvis? And I've already got plans for this weekend, I'm taking Lisa out to the lake, going to do some boating." John winces as he speaks.

"Watch ESPN this next Saturday, the 22nd and you'll see. I'm going to be dressed up like your Daddy at the bowl game with Boise State, only thing is I'll have blue hair. I've a seat in the front row," I boasted.

I left without a word on the subject of the other novel which is this novel that you are now reading.

Silent is what I remained and entered softly into my realm of words, where I am not judged immediately and where another Corona and tequila readily welcome me.

December 17th, 2012; 10:12 pm

Quietly I enter the garage. I was only going to be gone for a couple of hours, that is what I had promised Connie. She had returned home from work and we were thinking that a publication session would take place with Randi T. of AuthorHouse for the Children's book. I had left several messages earlier for her during the day, the Friday before and I was getting increasingly frustrated. On my last message, I left, "Please let us know if the text needs to be on the pictures." The message I received was, "Rico, so glad you are ready to publish, unfortunately, my hours are from 8 – 5pm EST, but please send me by email your entries.

"What the fuck?" I said loudly to myself as I dialed her number once again. "This is insane, I've paid, I left phone messages for several different days and I've only talked to the 'welcome me' operator of the AuthorHouse family.

December 18th, 2012;

My phone buzzed, picked it up off the table laying next to my laptop, I read the text and grinned. Wow, I am truly back with the story and continued to tap letters that formed into words that led into sentences that begat paragraphs that filled pages that finished chapters that eventually would create a book. This was my first day of vacation and I had through January 1st, 2013 to write at will, in the morning, at midday, in the afternoon, early evening, late night or early in the morning and then repeat at my own convenience.

December 18th, 2012; 10:02 am "It was fun yesterday looking forward to more. Have a great trip …Let me know what u need from me to get going on the book.." JS

I remember later, the importance of the day, "Today is my Goddaughter Paris' birthday. I must give her a call and send her best wishes on Facebook."

December 19th, 2012; Late afternoon

My car of which I am maneuvering pulls into a residential area of Chandler, AZ and into a driveway behind my Goddaughter Paris who has just pulled in ahead of me and is carrying a pizza into the house. She sees me and waits for me as I put my vehicle into park, shut off ignition, unhook my seatbelt and open the door. Paris sets the pizza on the trunk of her car and I give her a big hug, wish her a Happy Birthday and ask to see her new engagement ring. Proudly, she displays her young, delicate, left hand with the diamond arc around her third finger.

I missed her Birthday, by one day; but it was not based on the fact that I had forgotten, no it was because Julie her mother, TJ her brother and Bernard, her Grandfather, and I were waiting for Tom R., Paris' dad to return to the U.S. from Bejing, China. Tom works and lives in China as his employer is located there and the arrangements are not ideal with him being away from his family for a month or months at a time, but it is necessary. TJ has entered high school and has lived in the same area since his birth, Paris is an excellent interior design student at Arizona State with straight As on her report cards. She has lived in Arizona all of her days except the first month of life when she was born in England and then brought back to Arizona to begin her journey towards becoming a young woman. Julie has her employment and her motherly duties, so when times were tough for work in Arizona and the U.S., Tom had taken the job abroad as Captain for a private company flying their jet, their employees, their clients and their guests around the world. Tom had just arrived from Los Angeles via Bejing and was one day later than originally planned as he had of late been scheduled to fly his employer to L.A. instead of just catching a ride over. He had been in the left seat of the cockpit and was in charge of the jet, so an extra day's responsibility of refueling and getting the plane to a hanger had taken place.

This family which is an extended family to me is one that I don't get to see nearly as often as I wish. Maybe once, perhaps twice a year we get together, usually around the holidays, but, it is always as if all of us had just gathered together the previous day. My story, or I should state our story of when we met is somewhat comical, somewhat serious, but I would say it was in the Divine Plan of Schemes, I now have a lovely Goddaughter because of a poisonous Arizona scorpion.

A few fun places to visit in Cave Creek Arizona;
Harold's Corral, Buffalo Chip, Tap Haus & Hideaway Grill.

Amigo Mark B., owner of the Hideaway Grill.

Connie & Rico at the Hideaway Grill, somewhere in Cave Creek Arizona.

Rico & Mark H. enjoying Cruz Tequila.

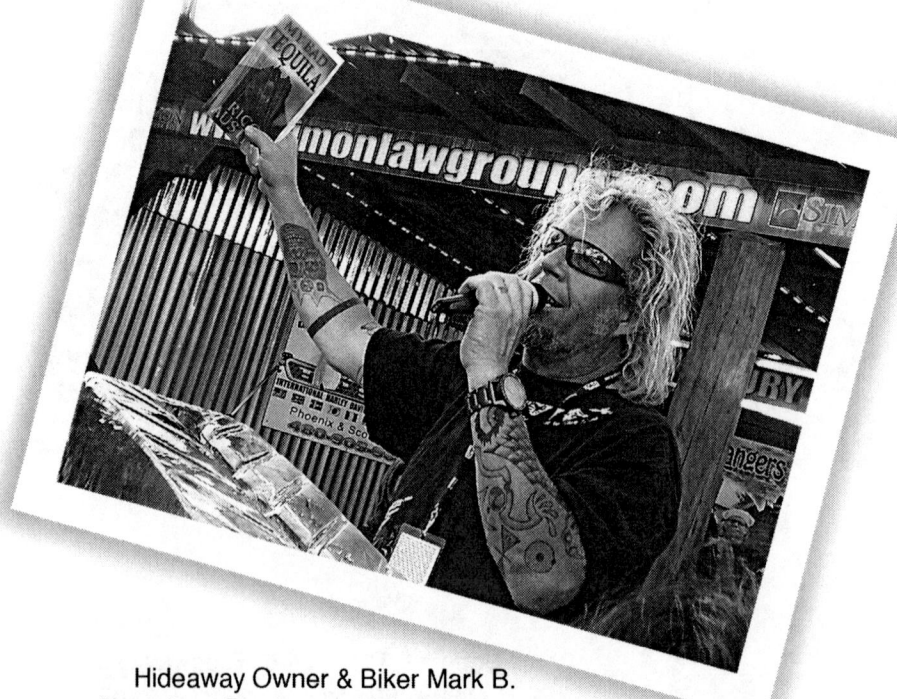

Hideaway Owner & Biker Mark B.
telling about Rico's novel "My Bad Tequila."

Rico, John, Diana, Mark, Dawn, Kari
and Rick in front row at the Hideaway Grill.

Chapter 11
Mountains to Desert

March, 1991;

It was in the first days of March 1991 when I moved from the higher elevation of Boise, Idaho to the desert of Mesa, Arizona. Perfect time to leave Idaho as snow was still aplenty on the ground and my 1978 Ford Granada did not have many more days to live or miles to give. This would be its final road trip and so I made the most of getting her packed to the fullest, as I knew chances were strong that I would not be returning to Idaho in the near future, perhaps, never again to reside. My bronze Granada had pretty much given up its spirit between Vegas and Wickenburg on Highway 93, it was using up to 4 quarts of oil every five miles or so and it looked like a locomotive train steaming through the desert with a cloud of smoke trailing me so close that there was no doubt where the darkish blue, heavy residue of smoke was coming from. However, I did have a plan, thanks in great part by my amigo Rich Collins of Eagle, a town just on the outskirts of the Boise community. He had seen the warning signs of age beginning to take its toll on my beloved Granada and had begged me to purchase AAA Auto Insurance in case of any breakdowns. Well, there were several, the first in Ely, Nevada of which an able bodied mechanic without much grease on his hands had my vehicle ready the next day. (For more detailed and fun information on this trip, please read "My Bad Tequila.")

Now, I'm on Highway 93, just miles away from Old Route 66, out of stock on oil that I had purchased in great bulk at Checker Auto or Pep Boys or….. I hitchhike the few miles back to Kingman, the town infamous for being the hideout and where most of the planning of bombing the Alfred P. Murrah Federal Building in Oklahoma City on April 19th, 1995 took place by domestic terrorists, Timothy McVeigh, Terry Nichols and Michael Fortier. This was four years prior to that Oklahoma City bombing, the attack that killed 168 people, including 19 children in the daycare center and injured over 800 innocent victims. Kingman had not gained its national infamous notoriety at this time.

I made a call to AAA at a phone booth, purchased a few more gallons of oil and was taken by tow truck back to the vehicle and hauled for exactly 100 miles before being unhitched and left alone again, in the desert. Just a tired, worn out car and a young man looking for a new start in the old west. I felt proud of myself, I had spent the extra $20 or so and had bought the premium package with the Automobile Association Club which included at no extra charge, 100 miles of towing. With a great new outlook on life, I popped the hood, unscrewed the oil cap and poured nearly 5 quarts of the life blood back into the Granada. I was back in business for a few more miles. Hobbling on four, worn, bald tires and several tens of quarts of oil I made it to Wickenburg and called AAA. This time the truck took me to Rick Dancer's apartment in Mesa, AZ arriving at around 2:00 am with a not too quiet way of releasing my dependable transportation into the parking lot. A few dog barks later, some neighbors cussing, Rick coming out in shorts, without a shirt nor shoes to greet me and I was to begin my life and adventures in Arizona.

You, the reader may be asking yourself, what about the scorpion, what about Paris. Well, hold on, because we are nearly there.

May, 1991;

I had just entered my apartment after a pleasant, but somewhat hot day at the community pool. Drying off and reaching for a fresh, clean pair of undershorts I glanced out the bedroom window as I heard screaming sirens that seemed to be turning into the complex. What in the ….., my mind raced as I fumbled to dress rapidly as done by Speedy Gomez, the rat in the cartoon.

With a pair of khaki shorts, a tee shirt and boating deck shoes that I managed to slip my feet into, I dashed out the door to tackle the flight of concrete stairs to get a closer view of where the action might be. While exiting the door I saw four, sturdy firemen enter the apartment below me. As I haphazardly missed two steps, catching myself on the third from the top step I thought to myself, "Slow down, maybe it's not that bad." I was extra worried and anxious to see what had happened to Julie or Paris.

No sooner had I entered the door jamb and crossed the threshold, I was met by a medic asking who I was. "Rico, I'm the upstairs neighbor, what, what has happened?" I stammered.

"We received a 911 call and Julie a resident here has been stung by a scorpion and has had an allergic attack. Do you know this person?"

"Yes, yes, of course, Julie lives here, she's from England and her husband is a pilot from Chicago." At this moment I thought of the six month old baby girl that was the joy and the light of Tom and Julie. "Is the baby, Paris, is she alright?"

"Yeah, the little girl is okay and doing fine, other than being scared to death by all the commotion and us firemen. She is still screaming, do you think you can calm her?"

"I'll try," and I ushered myself into the 1500 square foot household and followed the baby's endless wails to the bedroom.

"Hey there, Paris, Paris, please don't cry," I soothed with words as soft as I had ever spoken as I picked the little angel from her crib. I saw Julie briefly, being lifted onto a white linen stretcher as I moved swiftly to try and quiet to the bawling, hysterical baby.

Julie had been put into the ambulance that had just arrived and I still held the crying baby. I followed the firemen out the door as they made their way to the red truck filled with ladders and hoses. "What, what should I do with the baby?" I pleaded for explanations as I continued to rock her and softly pat her back.

"Any relatives around here?" the mustached one asked.

"I'm not sure, no I don't think so, other than her husband Tom, he is on a trip to Hong Kong, works for America West as a pilot captain. I don't have any idea when he'll return home. What should I do?" I helplessly begged for an acceptable answer.

Mr. Moustache, slowly raised his hand, looking as if thinking heavily, rubbed the heavy hair that covered his lip and stated, "Looks as if you'll be caring for the youngster."

"I have to work tomorrow, I have a date later this evening, I ......"

"Well, looks like a change of plans. You are taking care of this infant," and he joined the others in the truck, leaving me alone with a six month old child on my shoulder, neighbors near the door and a mind of bewilderment scanning my past.

I cared for that baby for two and one half days. I had some experience of changing diapers, heating milk in bottles and singing lullabies to my four, younger brothers. There were less than seven years in between the oldest, being me and the youngest, being Steven with David, Michael and Samuel taking the other three center slots.

The first thing I did was to pull all the blankets and pillows off the spare bed and put them down on the carpet in front of the television. Perhaps the diversion of commercials, dramas, daytime soap operas and game shows would soften the blow to a young girl having her mother whisked away in a white and red van with lights. After a couple hours the TV therapy started working and I called my employer to try and explain that I would be babysitting an infant for who knows how long and answer questions such as, "No, I'm not in jail and I'm not on drugs." I finally ended the conversation with, "This is my story and I'm sticking with it. Now, I've got to go, the baby is crying." Luckily, I was the top salesperson in my department so I was given the benefit of doubt and welcomed with open arms upon my return to the hard drive and computer sales world in Tempe.

Tom returned home, then Julie returned home and finally I returned home after another day of having to be in Paris' eyesight at all times during her waking hours She had suffered such dramatic trauma, that now I was her "momma," and she screamed each time I tried to leave. Eventually, she became reacquainted to her previous life before "Uncle Rico," and I too became reacquainted with my previous life before the "Baby Paris."

About three years later, I was invited by Tom and Julie to Paris' baptism in the Chicago suburbs and was chosen as little Paris' Godfather. This is a title and responsibility I still cherish and hold.

Rico with Baby Paris.

Rico with teenage Paris, Senior Prom night.

161

Chapter 12
VEGAS Baby!

December 20th, 2012;

"Vegas BABY!" I exclaim to myself as my right hand struggles to touch my left eye to wipe away the sleep. Damn, my arm still feels distraught, weak and foreign. I grimace and smile, "Vegas and my amigos are only a few hours away." My first cousin Susan is celebrating her day of birth on this day, she is only six months younger than what I was six months ago. We've known each other for a half a century now and perhaps I've missed wishing her a "Happy Birthday" six times or less as she has done for me. "Better dial her number before you forget," I reminded myself as I reached for the cell phone that was fully charged and still plugged into the outlet via small cord.

"Hello, you have reached the voice mail of Susan, please leave a message and I will return your call as soon as possible," is what I heard.

"Feliz Cumpleanos a ti, Feliz Cumpleanos a ti, Feliz Cumpleanos a ti----, Feliz Cumpleanos a ti', hello Susan, Happy Birthday, I hope you enjoy your day."

Bags were packed the night before, cowboy boots stored in the back seat on the floor; I was ready for Vegas and I hoped Vegas was ready for me.

Wickenburg is a town that you've read about at the beginning of this story. Wickenburg is indeed a "Cowboy town," and this is where an old roommate of mine had decided to make his home after 30 years in the Phoenix metro area and before that, Massachusetts. I was not on a tight schedule, I had time to see my old amigo Bob, to say hello, and to get the hell out, as each time he was a little shorter, a little paler, a little weaker; but, full of watered down vinegar. He was only a shadow of his former self.

Bob is in as good of spirits as a soul can hope to be, given his condition and take on life at the age of 74. Each time I see him, he is shorter, he is weaker and he seems to be more in tune with death. I remind myself to say only complimentary things, positive words, phrases and not to bring up the Mayan Calendar even though it be heavy upon my mind. Traveling to Vegas when the possibility of the end of the universe and mankind is upon us is not the most pleasurable thought, if you have a conscious at all.

Later that afternoon around 5:00 pm, I pulled into the parking lot of Harrah's Hotel and Casino and checked in. As I was waiting in line behind an Asian group that didn't seem to be speaking English, only Korean or Japanese or Filipino or …

"Hey buddy," I recognized the voice, "Vegas, BABY!" I turned and saw Rich Collins with his luggage and waved him in line to wait and check in with me.

"Already saw your customer and ready to partaay?" I high fived him as he pardoned and excused his way through the impatient line. "Wow, doesn't it feel good that neither of us has to work tomorrow? Usually when we're in Vegas, one of us has to get up early to see a customer or have a phone conference or go to a tradeshow," I reminded us both of how fortunate we were and what a great weekend was within view of our sights.

Rich and I were the best of friends, I had stood by his side when he married his only love, Rhonda in October 1991. I had moved to Phoenix earlier that year and had to return to Idaho for Best Man responsibilities. Then 13 years later, he returns the favor to me and waits on my left side while my bride to be was on my right.

We had met in a nightclub, Whiskey River in Boise in the early eighties. Both of us were students at Boise State University and much younger in those glory years.

I was working part time as a waiter / bouncer at Whiskey River; but, the night I met Rich, I had gotten off work early so was there to enjoy the women and the great rock 'n' roll bands that use to frequent that music house of memory. Rich had come in later as he worked for a local grocer part time and too, wanted to listen to 'Bates Motel,' a local band, crank it up. Towards the close of the night, Rich had come up to me and said, "I hear you play baseball for the Toronto Blue Jays, glad to meet you, Rich Collins is my name," and he offered his hand.

"Rico Austin, glad to meet you and no, I don't play for the Toronto Blue Jays," I chuckled and then continued, "just using that line along with a few others to try and get laid. I work here part time and at a Mexican restaurant called El Charro. I also go to school across the Boise River at the University. I'm on the football squad there, but some of the co-eds have a problem with football players so just using a different angle for getting pussy."

There is a little more to the story, however, that will most likely come out during the sequel to "My Bad Tequila," after I'm finished with this story and two others I am working and writing simultaneously on.

December 21st, 2012;
Alone in bed somewhere in a Harrah's hotel room and sometime around noon, I think;
"Geez my fucking head is pounding," I blurt out loud enough so that Rich can hear me in the adjoining room as I could hear him singing his favorite Mexican tune that we had all sang together, on vacation, in Cabo San Lucas about six years earlier. It goes something like this, "Ole, ole, ole, ole, oleoleole, ole, ole, o-le, o-le, ole, ole … and on and on and just goes on until I don't ever what to hear the two syllable word of O-LE ever again.

Rich had asked me the evening before if we could drop off his rental car the next day after some Christmas shopping at the factory outlet mall. "Juicy Couture" was the store of choice for Rich to be shopping for his bride of twenty one years and I was along for the fun. I had never been to "Juicy Couture" nor did I know what kind of store it was; I figured it to be either a candy store or sexual toy store for adults. Turns out to be sweat suits or sweat outfits whichever word is preferred, also scarves, purses and some inexpensive jewelry. When Rich and I hang out together, whether it is going through a fast food drive thru, grabbing a beer or in this case shopping, we always try and make it loads of entertainment for ourselves and those around us. As we entered the store with hangovers as dramatic as our Christmas shopping dreams we were met with kind, welcoming hellos.

"Hey Connie might like something from here," Rich suggested.

"Yeah, that was what I was thinking," I said, after getting over my shock of no chocolates or edible panties to eat. "The only thing she has told me that she wants me to get for her is an Everlast stand up punching bag that she saw at Bed, Bath and Beyond. It reminds me of those old Bozo the clown punching bags that we had as a kid. She gave me a picture of it from their ad and a 15% off coupon. If we see one of those stores here, I'd like to stop, get it and take it home with me."

"No problem, hey here's something that I think Rhonda would like,"

Rich says as he holds up a small, dark blue, set of pants and top.

I give Rich a quick wink and say, "Amigo, watch this," as I pick up a size small bright orange outfit and make my way to one of the young, female store clerks near the counter.

"Where's your dressing room?" I asked casually.

"Uh, it's, it's over there," she pointed nervously, not quite sure how to react.

"Thanks," I said, and disappeared after hearing Rich's laughter in the distant background.

"That was great, did you see the look on that poor girl's face," Rich asked.

"Yeah, I've got one more that I'll ask the other girl near the door," as I grabbed an XXXL sized, pink sweat suit combo.

"Hi, do you think my Grandmother would like this color?" as I pulled the waist out wide to show exactly how super large these bottoms were.

"Um, yeah, maybe, is that the right size?" she questioned nervously.

"Well, actually if you have something a bit larger that would be great," I stammered, trying to sound embarrassed about the entire situation.

"I think that is the largest size that we carry," she said, trying to be as helpful and professional as possible.

"Maybe, it will work," as I pulled, inspected and stretched at the clothing to get it to look a size larger. "My granny likes to try and look sexy, so if it's tight and shows off her bosom I'm sure she won't mind too much. She's looking for husband numero cinco," I flirted playfully, while adding a bit of Espanol to my repertoire to show added sophistication to my sentence.

"Well, I'm sure this outfit will do the trick. You are such a nice guy to be so concerned with getting your Grandmother a nice gift," she pleasantly said.

"Yeah, thanks, I'm trying to get her hitched so she doesn't have to sleep on my couch much longer. You should hear her ass snore, unbelievable, sounds like a fricking freight train. Know of any old dudes that want a full sized and experienced old lady that is a great cook and knows how to clean fish?" I added as I heard Rich snicker, hidden from view on the other side of the aisle.

"Uh, no, I don't think so, um, I need to go get some more merchandise from the backroom, please excuse me,'" she apologized as she quickly moved away from me and left the scene of a place she didn't want to be.

Rich came from his hiding place, we both had a good laugh and then bought our wives matching outfits at a great discounted, two for one price. We made a pact, not to mention the bargain we had achieved in mixed company, not ever.

"Time for a drink after all that tough shopping," and I pointed towards the parking garage.

We were sitting at the 'Yard House' a couple hours later, downing a cold, tasty cerveza when an older, white haired, tall gentleman with an athletic build sitting next to me started a conversation, "You look very familiar, you're someone famous, aren't you?" he accused in a good natured manner.

"I don't know about famous, but I'm an author and a fairly well known blogger. Rico Austin is my name, and this next to me is Mr. Rich Collins. Glad to meet you, we're out here for the MAACO Bowl game between the Boise State and Washington football teams."

"Hi, I'm Robert Foust and here's my card, I'm a bail bondsman, so if you boys get into any trouble, give me a call. I've got a few stories that I've written that would be great movie material. I was a fighter pilot in the Vietnam War, also spent time in prison for smuggling, played some professional baseball years ago, stuff like that."

"Wow, sounds like my kind of stories," I congratulated him and shook his hand in appreciation for serving in the armed forces.

"Would you want to read any of these stories? Perhaps, you could write one of my wild experiences someday, what do you think?"

"Sure, I'd like to see what you have; but, I have three other projects I need to put to rest first. I'm writing quite a story right now about Elvis's legitimate, illegitimate son. I'm telling John Dennis Smith's story, so if you're in no rush then maybe late this next year or early 2014," I offered.

"Have you a card or anything where I can contact you?" Robert asked.

"Yes, here's my email address. Send me an email and I'll give you my mailing address," I replied as I handed him my card.

"Thanks, I'll send you an email and then I'll probably mail you the story about smuggling drugs in Canada. Nice to have met you and I can't wait to read your novel "My Bad Tequila," he closed in conversation.

"Sounds great and don't hold your breath in getting a phone call from us, our wives will kick our asses if we end up in a Vegas jail," I chuckled as I shook his manicured hand once again.

"Hey, I just got a text from Emilio, he's at the Luxor and wants to know when we're going to meet tonight." I read from my phone as I finished the conversation with my new friend named Robert from Las Vegas.

Rich and I left to retrieve the Blu Kaboy.

"How's it going amigo," I greeted VooDoo Daddy as he opened the door to my car awaiting outside the valet and drop off area, out front of the Luxor.

"Que pasa Compadre," he returned the greeting as we gave each other a big, brotherly hug. "I've got the Elvis costumes for you and Rich. Want to go try them on?"

"Absolutamente," was my final answer as I put the car in gear, headed towards the Embassy Suites on Swenson Street, right behind the Hard Rock Casino and Hotel. Rich and I had checked out of Harrah's late that morning and had claimed another hotel as our party headquarters. I had a certificate that was about to expire for two nights in a suite and it was located next to Boise State's football events being held at the Hard Rock. Many of the alumni, boosters and the BSU football squad were staying there, so it was very convenient. Add that, with the bonus of a nightly, hosted, happy hour and made to order omelettes for breakfast and our plan was ideal. We tried on the outfits. I decided to wear my Blue Elvis outfit and Rich put his civilian clothing back on his body, we had some free cocktails in the lounge where we met a couple of the ESPN camera crew that would be working the game. We asked them to join us on the short walk to the Hard Rock where we had been invited to the Varsity B party at one of the smaller bars where the Athletic Director and other BSU brass would be introduced. The Blue Elvis attire was a gigantic hit and pictures galore were taken. I even got one picture taken with Coach Chris Peterson (Coach Pete) and starting quarterback, Joe Southwick with his mustache that he hadn't shaven for a few games due to a winning streak, unfortunately, the look was that of an eighties porn star, but athletes are superstitious, so I had to agree with his taken position of not shaving until after the game. I have to say that I was very impressed with Joe, quite a nice, polite kid. This quarterback had one of the most difficult jobs in all of college football, he had come in after the most winning quarterback in college football history. He was the quarterback that came into lead the Broncos after Kellen Moore, who had won 50 games in his college career with only three losses. He had broken Texas Longhorn, Colt McCoy's record of 45 wins by an NCAA Division I FBS quarterback. Yes, Joe had some huge shoes to fill and pulled those shoe laces tight like a man and led his team to an 11 win season.

We enjoyed a few more cocktails and pictures, then the three of us hailed a cab and had the driver drop us off at Harrah's to which we caught the escalator upward and strode into Toby Keith's 'I Love this Bar.'

We were met by an unfriendly, concerned, security guard that needed to see my identification as he did not see the humor of a Blue Elvis entering the establishment. The costume consisted of wide style, orange sunglasses, a blue wig, an orange scarf, a couple of big ass, blue, diamond looking rings and a blue and white jumpsuit that is very difficult to get in and out of. Bathroom breaks need to be scheduled very carefully, so when the overzealous security guard in the bright yellow, polo shirt wanted to see my ID which was in my Levi back pocket, under the jumpsuit, I had to nearly take the entire thing off and I was not wearing a shirt. Unfortunately, my fifty something body resembles Elvis' figure when he was in his forties, so not a real glamorous shot. Why didn't this happen to me in my twenties and thirties when I would have gladly shown my six pack abs and cut chest. Now, I have a baby keg for a gut and a stuffed ice chest. I finagled and found my wallet, presented my license and took my wig off momentarily to show my bartender friend, Leo that is was me, Rico, the corona and margarita drinking dude. While I was reaching in my back pocket, partially clad, Rich had taken a snapshot of the security guard and me. After receiving clearance, the entire gang posed with Blue Elvis for a photo, including a now, smiling security guard, a female bartender, BSU Pimp Daddy and a drunk, Canadian cowboy from Alberta ruining the photo op by flipping the bird with his middle finger. Another great night of not much rest.

December 22nd, 2012;

Game day has arrived and so has the two Blue Elvi and VooDoo Daddy into the parking lot of Sam Boyd Stadium on the outskirts of Vegas. It was great fun posing with all the Boise State fans and having the Washington Husky fans asking if we would stand with them for a photo. Lots of good will toward all football fans, including those of the Las Vegas Running Rebels that were there for a good day of gridiron football watching. That night, Rich and I went clubbing, sans the Elvis costumes. I thought briefly about my circumstance of being stuck with the needle and wondered how many more trips to Vegas were in my future. For once in my life I did not want to be recognized, just to people watch, to have a margarita, lean against the bar and enjoy the dueling pianists playing at 'New York, New York Piano Bar'. Tomorrow would come soon and I'd be driving back on that lonesome highway to Scottsdale.

December 23rd, 2012;

I'm cruising through Boulder, Nevada when I receive a text from Blu Kaboy, "Compadre, we made the front page of the Las Vegas Review Journal." I pull into Terrible's gas station and sure enough, in bright orange, blue and white, the three of us are in full color on the Sunday's edition of the LVRJ. Centered on the front page we were, with title stating, "FOOTBALL FANS WITH LAS VEGAS FLAIR." I picked up 3 copies, gave the clerk her $6.00 and headed across the new Hoover Dam bypass, the Mike O'Callaghan – Pat Tillman Memorial Bridge. If you know me personally, then you know, Mr. Pat Tillman is my hero.

December 24rd, 2012;

As I make my way to the building with signage that reads Bed, Bath and Beyond, I hope to goodness there is one more Everlast punching bag available or I might as well go back to Vegas. All I could find was the store model, so I went ahead and asked a floor person for help and behold, one last box was located and sold to me. I had the "Juicy Couture" wrapped package and now the main event. "Next year, I'm not going to wait until Christmas Eve to shop," I promised myself. At least I didn't have to risk my gifts getting discovered because of being poorly hid. We opened the gifts that evening, gave thanks for Baby Jesus and life was good. I had many more bowl games to watch on television in the coming days.

Blue Elvi &
VooDoo Daddy
at MAACO Bowl.

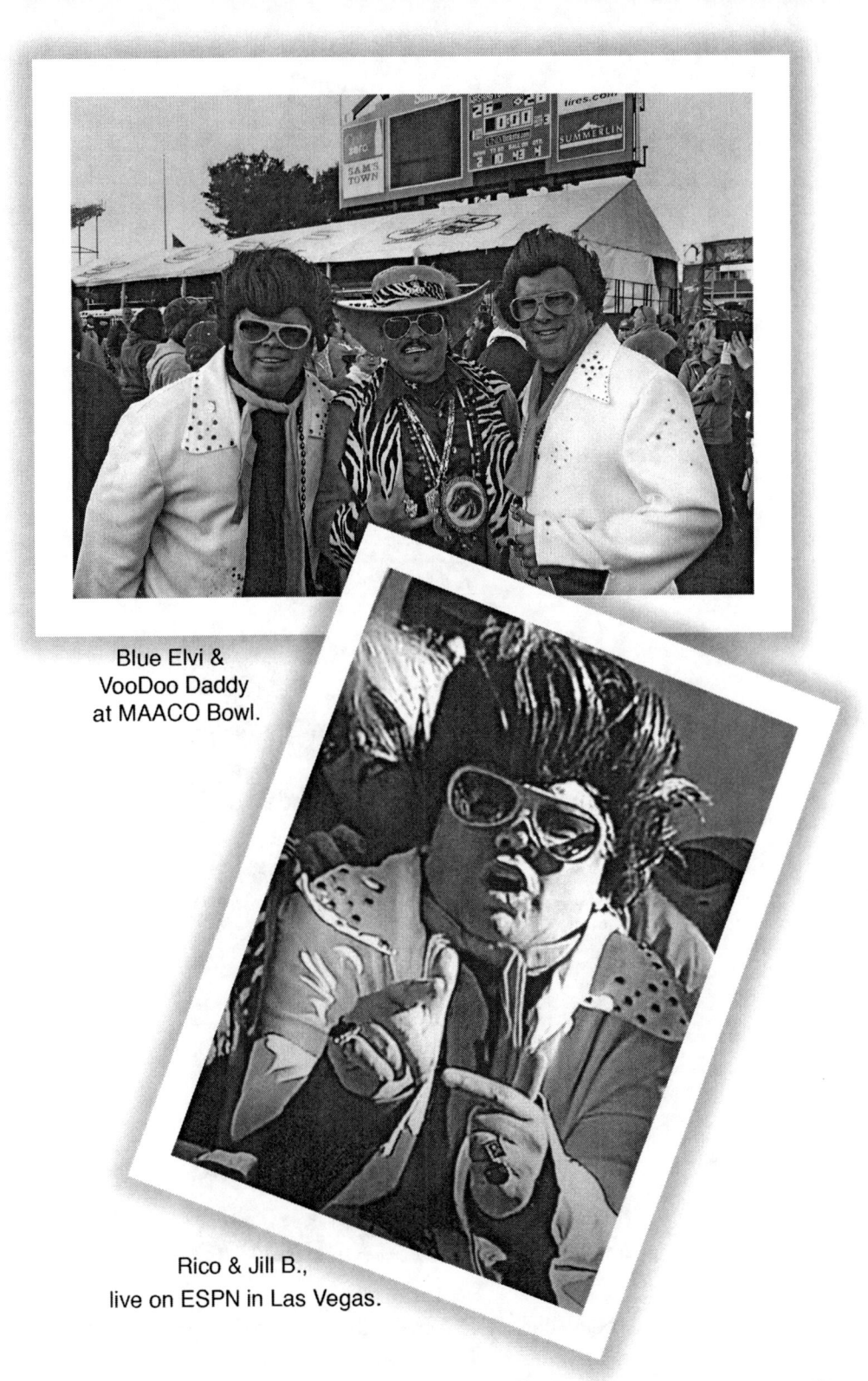

Rico & Jill B.,
live on ESPN in Las Vegas.

After being carded at Toby Keith's, "I Love This Bar" in Las Vegas.

Only in Vegas - Blue Elvis, Mr. & Mrs. Santa Claus, Blu Kaboy & Katy Perry ? with her blue hair.

Emillo, Rich, Elf, Rico & Michel
at MAACO Bowl.

Blue Elvi & Blu Kaboy are Rockin' in Vegas;
front page of the Las Vegas Review Journal.

174

Chapter 13
Post Vegas

From: Cindy Work
Subject: Book
To: Rico Austin
Date: Thursday, December 27, 2012, 12:01 pm

Hello, Christmas Eve we had friends and family over, and passed around the Book to gather feedback. After taking notes and critiques we sat down tonight to review. The highlighted writings are those we made, trying to create a flow and keeping the story consistently written in one perspective. We wanted to send it to you both to review before we meet on Thursday. This is your idea and story. These are our suggestions. See you around 1 at Artisan. Cin

December 28th, 2012;
I wake up, tired again and don't know or understand why. I decide to put Connie's punching bag together, but, don't have any sand to keep the base heavy when landing flurries of punches so that the entire contraption does not fall over. I send a birthday remembrance to my deceased dad on Facebook.

December 29th, 2012;
Again tired, don't feel refreshed and the wife asks me if I would please join her to Home Depot for sand and Walmart to get various products and food to keep me interested in life for another week.

Another horrible review of "My Bad Tequila" on Amazon.com, again from a woman that seems obsessed with hatred, vile and venom. The funny thing, not hilarious; but, a bit strange is that I have had three horrific reviews in the last two months and before that a string of nine, great, five star reviews. The bad reviews are as if the "church women" giving them have not even read the book, because of what they write in the review, doesn't even take place in the novel. What happened to the Commandment, "Thou shalt not bear false witness?" Another old fashioned case of hypocrisy. I look into it, as I have amigos that are gurus with computers, they find that all three, plus one earlier have one thing in common ..... now, I know that I have been played. We take a look into the past, which is more shaded than mine, and everything is clear.

I'm in a sour mood, so after assembling the punching bag and filling the base with sand, I print out a picture of Lou Holtz and Mark May and attach their ugly mugs to the bag. Lou Holtz, once a respected coach of Notre Dame, Arkansas and Minnesota, now is a wind bag announcer and sports anal-yst for ESPN and CBS sports. Mark May a former college and professional football player also has the same late career path as does Lou Holtz with ESPN. Of the many reasons I don't care for either of these anal-ysts (I have this word broken down in syllables for personal reasons) is that both of them have a strong dislike for the Boise State University football team and bad mouth the WAC league, the Mountain West league or any other league that BSU is in, or considers joining.

I have Connie take a couple of snapshots of me posing with the enemies of the Bronco Nation, post them on Facebook for my amigas and amigos of Idaho and then I take a couple of good jabs and one good, full round house kick to the faces of Lou and Mark. I hear a faint hissing noise and watch as the air slowly exits through a tiny hole created from my pummeling the pictures. This Christmas present lasts for less than one round.

Connie now has a credit at Bed, Bath and Beyond as there is no fricking way in heck that I am going to put another one of these cheap (Everlast - my ass) bags together again. A good sturdy jump rope will be a good replacement for any needed aerobic exercise. I probably won't be meeting Muhammad Ali or Mike Tyson in the ring anytime soon.

December 30th, 2012; 1:19 am

Connie tells me she has to go to bed as I beg her to have one more drink with me before leaving me alone at the kitchen table. Alone once more with my laptop, a bit of Merlot wine and a refrigerator full of Corona light beer. I open another Corona, cut a jagged slice of lime and push it through the opening. Connie has been tremendous throughout this ordeal with the book and even more so with "the incident" in San Francisco. We have not engaged in any sexual activity for over two months, I have held her, gave her good night kisses and good morning hugs; but, nothing more.

She used to tell me quite often of all the memoirs, the short stories, the blogs, that never a love note have I written for her. My reply had been, "Babe, no need as I can always call and talk with you; if I did not have that luxury, then lover letters from me you would receive."

She backed down, smiled and replied, "I guess you are off the hook as I never thought of it that way."

It does seem the right time, at this hour to write her the love letter she has so long awaited, even though she must share it, as the entire world can read it, if and when they should get to this passage in my memoir. I hope that she will forgive me for putting it out there in front of mankind, but I feel it important to let others know and see that perhaps he or she should write a letter of thanks or an old fashioned letter of love to his or her significant other.

"Dearest Connie," on second thought, maybe this is not such a fantastic idea. I already share so many personal thoughts and moments of our life that when I write her a love letter, it should be for her eyes only. I do hope you all will understand; however, I will share with you, her personal Elvis story. Remember, earlier I wrote, that most all of us have our own Elvis tale or memory that happened to us personally or to a member of our family. Well, my wife is one of the, "most of us."

It was early summer of 1972 and Connie was ten years of age. She and her brother Wade, younger by nearly two years; seven hundred and eighteen days to be exact, had both worked on the 660 acres that made up the T. family farm ever since they were old enough to walk and carry a quart filled, plastic bottle of milk to feed the newborn calves and lambs in the spring. More times than not during this time of year there was still snow on the ground and the wind was sharp with a lasting bite. Winters were long in Northern Minnesota, the long, cold months stretched sometimes from late September in the autumn until early May in the spring.

Summers were a welcome sight and this summer was no different. Connie and Wade had finished their morning chores of feeding the animals and of milking the twenty one head of dairy cows. Their parents, like their parents before them were hard working farmers that toiled the rich, black soil which gave food to them and their animals in the late summer and early fall, enough to last another long, harsh winter. Most of the crops were sold to pay the mortgage, the taxes, to purchase next year's seed and to repair the farm implements as one more season was always needed for the machinery to withstand. A new, used tractor would have to wait for a couple more strong harvests as debt was a four letter word to this family and to most all of the other families spread throughout the county.

Chores complete, with mother and dad still laboring in the field before lunch time, had offered Wade and Connie a rare chance to watch their black and white RCA television set with its three channels, NBC (National Broadcasting Company), CBS (Columbia Broadcasting System) and ABC (American Broadcasting Company).

While they were relaxing and watching TV, an interesting advertisement caught Connie's eye and ear, "Special Offer, get your own private collection of Elvis songs," and continued, "don't worry about sending a check or money order, because, if you order COD, we'll throw in free delivery right to your doorstep. Please call this phone number to get started on having a full collection of Elvis Presley's hits delivered in four to five weeks."

Connie had heard the words free and COD. She asked her younger brother if he knew what COD was and of course he didn't; but, did encourage her to dial the number she had written down, the number that had been shown several times flashing on the television set that had been repeated even more times by the barking announcer. The two siblings had heard their Mother and Dad speak very highly of Elvis and they had heard him sing on the radio. They had seen him on the commercial and knew that Janis and Alvin would indeed be pleased with them for ordering it, especially since it was COD and free. Connie talked to the lady on the other end of the phone, had given the lady their complete address including rural route and the Elvis album would be on its way to Minnesota in just a few short weeks. "Let's surprise Mom and Dad, now promise that you won't tell," was the older girl's advice to the agreeing, younger, smiling boy.

A couple of weeks had gone by with long, summer days filled with work and not much play. A knock on the door and the mailman was waiting on the steps with a package. Connie and Wade had completely forgotten about that late morning in the small living room when a phone call to a distant place had been made. "Hello, Mrs. T., I have a package for you, it is COD and I need to collect $20.80 from you, for your order."

Wade and Connie looked at each other, fear stricken and the coloring of their faces were fading quickly as they left the scene when their mother went digging for coins in her purse. "I don't remember ordering anything, what is it?" she questioned while continuing to search for any money at all.

"Why it's a record album of course, must have been advertised on television. A phone call would have had to have been made to place the order," the postman went on talking.

"Okay, perhaps my husband ordered it, will you take a check?"

"Usually it's preferred that I get cash, but, since I know you and your family, sure. Please make the check out to this name as he laid the package on the kitchen dining table where Janis was filling in the blank lines on the check.

After Alvin had denied ordering the album, the two, too quiet children were called to the living room and shown the record. "Do either of you know anything about this?" Janis sternly questioned.

"She did it," Wade points at his older sister, while clearing his own name of any wrong doing.

"You said it was okay," Connie retorts back in self defense.

"Well, it is done and over with now, so you two are both grounded for a week, with no television privileges and that means on Saturday too, no cartoons. Do you both understand?"

Another month or so of summer eases by and on a humid, Saturday night a party is being held at the T. family farm. Connie is in bed with one of the worst ear infections and aches that she has ever encountered, while Wade is busy playing with his cousins and friends.

Janis and Alvin have decided to have a rare celebration and festivity of food, drink and music for their relatives, neighbors and friends. Everyone is enjoying themselves except for poor, ill Connie, who has to put up with the constant bass noise of the Elvis records and hearing the bap, bap, boom, boom of all party goers dancing on the linoleum kitchen floor to that COD record. Yes, Elvis Presley was a hit and his voice was played over and over and over that night in Northwestern Minnesota. Connie had told me that only her Uncle Wally had taken the time to come check on her, to see how she was doing that evening. Even her Aunt Dolores couldn't pull herself away from Elvis and his music, long enough to check on her favorite niece.

Like all good stories, at the time it seemed like the most awful occurrence; but, now, it is remembered with great satisfaction, a smile and a longing for those 'good ol' days' when Uncle Wally, Alvin and Janis were alive and able to listen and dance to Elvis Presley tunes.

December 30th, 2012; 4:21 am

I ease myself up from the chair of which I had been sitting while writing, I look at the green digital numbers on the microwave and decide it is time for me to close my eyes once again; to let the tiredness creep completely atop me and into me. I welcome the end of another day, even though it is the beginning of another day. As I open the refrigerator to open a pack of pepperoni slices, I wonder to myself, "When my time on earth is near the end, will I welcome death with open arms or will I curse the angels that come to take me away, asking for just one more day?" I must sleep.

Alarm, alarm, yes that is my alarm going off at 9:15 am; Need to be showered, dressed and out of the house headed to Desert Mountain by 10:00 am to meet the P. threesome. Kurt had emailed me five days earlier asking if I'd be able to join he, his dad - Lee and his brother - Rahn for a round of eighteen holes; we'd be playing at Cochise, one of the six courses that Desert Mountain living offered.

I was to meet the three of them at Rahn's home and then follow them over. But, Connie needed me to try and print something out on the printer from my laptop that she had sent via her MAC. No bueno. Time was ticking and nothing was moving ahead. I hopped in the car after stuffing the clubs, shoes and an extra glove into the trunk. Then flinging the front page of the Las Vegas paper, a picture that the Idaho Statesman had sent me of myself and a blue line of the children's book, "ARIZONA Is Where I Live," I headed East and then North.

"I'm running just a few minutes late, I'll meet you at the Cochise

Golf Course, should be there at 10:38 according to GPS," I explained to Kurt. Our tee time was etched on paper, 11:27 am and I did not want them waiting on me. When I pulled up, Rahn waved and beckoned me to the practice range. I pulled into the club drop area, clicked the button that opened the trunk, met the attendant and grabbed my shoes of golf.

"Hey Buddy, great to see you," Kurt's words rang true and delightful to my ears. Kurt was the first person I had met at Thunderbird School of Global Management. Kurt was then a dead ringer for actor William Hurt when Bill Hurt was a younger man. In August of 1996, Kurt had just arrived earlier that week in a maroon car from St. Louis near the Gateway Arch and was ready to have a drink or two, pizza and get to know his surroundings. That is how we met that first night, in the on-campus pub and have been great friends ever since.

Kurt had shared with me that first night, the story of arriving into Glendale, Arizona and how excited he had become as he neared his destination of a deepened learning for international finance and obtaining an MBA in two years of time. As he pulled into address of 1 Global Place that late August day in 1996, the campus looked as if a bomb during wartime had struck the entire surrounding area. Just days before on August 14th, wind gusts of 115 miles per hour had been recorded at Deer Valley Airport in North Phoenix which was approximately 12 miles from Thunderbird. Roof tiles, broken glass, air conditioning units, palm trees and large palo verde trees were strewn and lazily thrown about the school's acreage, greeting Kurt, other Americans from the 50 states and citizens from around the world, looking to better themselves by way of education in the Grand Canyon and Copper State of Arizona.

Connie's parents, Alvin & Janis.

Wade & Connie about this age when ordering the Elvis album, shown above.

182

Chapter 14
Cuba with Love

A trip to Jamaica with Kurt in March of 2001 that spurred a side trek to Cuba during the time that then, U.S. President George W. Bush was fining those running amok to Havana and all other villages on the Cuban island for disobeying the embargo set some fifty odd years ago in 1960; this being the same year I entered the world through an at home birth and became a United States Citizen. In that same year that Kurt and I visited Cuba, so had another couple of people. A month later, in April of 2001, a Port Huron, Michigan couple, Michael and Andrea McCarthy, went to Cuba through Canada. These devout Catholics had considered the trip a missionary effort, with a bit of vacation thrown in for good measure. They had brought medicine to a group of nuns in Havana and had joined them in religious services. The McCarthy's had done this same humanitarian act on similar trips to Haiti and Mexico. The fine total of $9,750 was substantially lower than the typical fine of $7,500 each for first-time offenders, according to the U.S. Department of Treasury's Office of Foreign Asset Control. The OFAC, had asked Administrative Law Judge Irwin Schroeder to fine the couple less than the ordinary fine in considering mitigating factors, including how much money they had spent in Cuba, and their true motives for visiting the island south of Key West. Judge Schroeder took into account a number of those factors in deciding the amount of the fine for Michael McCarthy, who is a physican's assistant and Andrea McCarthy a nurse. The most deciding factors were the humanitarian and religious intentions of the trip and the couple's limited ability and income to pay a substantial civil penalty as they had three university-aged students that they were helping support through college.

Upon entrance into the forbidden Cuba, I had asked the immigration officer to stamp my passport and he asked me if Spanish, "Estas segura?" translating to "Are you sure?"

"Si, si, por favor, estampa de Cuba en mi pasaporte," I answered nervously, not completely sure if I did indeed want the logo of the Cuban Island permanently etched in my passport as I still had to return back into my country upon returning back through Jamaica.

"Rico, are you fucking out of your mind?" a voice of reason, that of Kurt spoke with disbelief.

"Yes, perhaps so; but, this is a once in a lifetime opportunity and I may never return. I do want to have proof when others call bullshit on our visit," I tried frantically to reason the absurdity of my request.

The Cuban behind the desk on the stool grabbed the rubber inked stamp and slammed it onto one of my passport pages. It was done and now nothing I could do about it. Welcome to Cuba!

My interest in Cuba was twofold: I wanted to visit the bars, the restaurants, the streets, the marina and all of the other haunts of the great writer and sportsman, Mr. Ernest Hemingway. I longed to drink mojitos in Bodequita del Medio and sip on daiquiris in La Floridita, these Havana watering holes made famous by Papa. It was my dream to witness first hand, with my eyes a small plaque hanging in La Floridita with Hemingway's signed quote: "My mojito in the Bodeguita del Medio and my daiquiri in the Floridita." Secondly, I wished to converse in Spanish with the beautiful and American starved Cuban chicas. Yes, Americans are at a premium in Cuba, probably the only place where as a United States citizen you are looked at with such amazement and curiosity. Everywhere else in the world a North American U.S. traveler ventures, there are scornful glances of disdain, quietly whispered sarcasms, murmurings of hate for the red, white and blue star spangled banner with 13 stripes representing the British Colonies that declared independence from the Kingdom of Great Britain, becoming the first 13 states in the Union and the 50 stars representing the 50 states of the United States of America.

There were great things about Cuba and things that were sad near Havana. One thing I noticed quite frequently when walking through the city of Havana, along the malecon and visiting the Hotel National de Cuba that most of the visitors or tourists were male and the automobiles of Cuba were of the nineteen fifties. These traveling men were mainly from the three countries of Italy, Germany and France and were accompanied by young, light complected Cuban girls between ages of twelve and nineteen according to my undercover questions asked to the locals that knew of all things prostitutional and more. The lighter the skin and younger the female, the more expensive the rate of sexual intercourse. In poorer countries with less entrepreneurial opportunity and capitalism it seems to me that there is more free enterprise when it comes to sex, which is completely the opposite of what common sense would state. This being said, the young girls that sell their bodies must be extra careful not to be caught by the state officials and policia as it is an offense with set fines and prison sentences for both buyer (fucker) and buyee (fuckee). "In Cuba, legislation effective August 1997, sets fines, prison sentences of 2 to 5 years, or up to 8 years for public health, education, tourism, law enforcement or government officials and confiscation of property for pimps, madams and those who rent space out for prostitution." ("Cuba to crack down on abettors of prostitution," Reuters, 20 July 1997).

When gathering knowledge from the locals and talking with the exploited females, I found that most of the time each of the prostitutes had one thing in common, she could not make it to the end of the month with just her salary. That is the reason, she, decided to sell her body to tourists that welcomed the exploitation.

Years later, I talked with members from a Chilean soccer team that had visited Cuba to play 'Futbol' and when we were sharing stories of conquering worlds and women, one young Chilean athlete told of a ten year old girl trading her body for a water bottle with a foreign logo on it. I just about cried, hearing this tale while others laughed and joked at the great bargain the soccer player in his late teens to early twenties had scored at the price of a child losing her childhood. What a tragedy for a child to lose their virginity and begin their sexual lives at such an early and delicate age. A child should be having fun, playing kickball or hopscotch with friends, playing with dolls, not giving their temple of body away for food, money, water bottles or other worldly possessions; but, this is the cold reality. A term I coined and have the trademark rights, states, "Have a Double Shot of Reality." Do not forget how lucky you are to be able to read, to be able to make your own choices and to live a life of freedom.

Castro appears to be contributing to prostitution and the increase in prostitution tourism by his own tolerance. He remarked that Cuban women are prostitutes not because they needed to be but rather because they liked to make love, and that they are the most educated and the healthiest prostitutes on the market. (Jesus Zuniga, "Cuba: The Thailand of the Caribbean," Independent Journalists' Cooperative, 18 June 1998).

During our visit to Cuba, Kurt and I proudly and quietly helped the working class of Cubans by staying in the local neighborhoods and renting "Casa Particular" meaning "Private House" and not staying in the nationally owned hotels and in not participating in helping the government make more money. In 1997, the government allowed Cubans to rent out part of their homes, but within a year the local municipal officials determined that "casa particulares" were representing a threat to the hotel industry and passed laws and regulations forbidding the operation of these establishments. Had the owners been caught renting the entire house to us for only $20 per day they might have been fined a large sum of money and been sent to jail. We had to enter the house and leave the house stealthily and unnoticed by spying neighbors, school children and street food vendors. This was a worrisome task, knowing we might jeopardize someone's freedom including our own by not being alert and careful at all times when nearing the premises. We loved Cuba and the sincere, kind hearted Cuban Amigas and Amigos we met during our short and wonderful stay there.

VIVA CUBA!!!

Rico's passport with Cuba & Jamaica Stamps
also shown, T-Bird Ring.

Rico on the streets of Havana Cuba, with old cars.

Rico & Kurt at Nightclub with Locals in Havana.

Havana Public Transportation.

Havana Housing.

189

Chapter 15
Out with the Old, In with the New

December 31st, 2012;

I awake with pain in my right arm and left leg, lifting the sheet I manage to control my groan. "When the …. did I get this damn old?" is the first question of the last day of the old year in the beginning of the morning. I think slowly; yes, this reminds me of a song by Garth Brooks, "I'm much too young to feel this damn old" as I walk to the bathroom to relieve myself of a half night's piss buildup.

"Would this be my last year of celebrating the last day of any year?" This is nearly the same question I've asked myself for nearly every occurrence of significance since "the incident" in Frisco.

Had I seen Disneyland and Palm Springs for the last time in October? Would Mickey Mouse, Donald Duck and Marilyn Monroe be no more? Thoughts of mortality rolled through my mind at a greater speed than the "Silver Streak" barreling into the Chicago train depot. This 1976 action, comedy, thriller movie starring Gene Wilder and Richard Pryor was one of my favorites and I smiled thinking about the craziness of the scenes that raced through my memory. I was a young man then, nearly within a year of finishing up my studies at Marsing High School in Idaho. Alas, I was sad no more and enjoyed the colder than usual day.

Connie arrived later in the day, filled with good spirits of leaving the year 2012 and anxious to celebrate the coming of year 2013. "Where are we going tonight?' she sounded off as a youngster asking her parents.

"Hadn't given it much thought, h'mm, how about Pinnacle Peak? We went there last year and had a grand time."

"Yes, that sounds great, how about going around sevenish?"

"Let's just go for a couple of drinks and get an appetizer or two and bring one back, one for me and one for you," stated I, confidently and enthusiastically.

A few minutes before seven and my ass is killing me, still my stomach has not returned to normal since "the occurrence and the medication." Hemorrhoidal Ointment by Preparation H or Equate still spells relief for hemorrhoids on steroids. If you've ever encountered this uncomfortable subject and feeling then you'll most likely be chuckling; however, if your hemorrhoids have never betrayed your butt and stayed where they should stay put, then you may be wondering why in the heck is this crazed writer babbling on about it. This is the secret, if you've had to use the ointment to prevent further irritation, then it is no big deal; but, if you've never experienced the pain, the suffering, the humiliation, then your time may be nigh, so don't think you and your asshole are above this lowly discussion.

January 1st, 2013; late morning

John texts me, "I'm singing at Greasewood Flats between 2 – 4"

I reply, "Wish I would have known, heading into Cave Creek with out of town friends from St. Louis and Anthem!"

January 1st, 2013; 3:05 pm

"I'm hoping the Rose Bowl game will be a good one, but I'm afraid Stanford will run all over Wisconsin," I analyzed to Kurt as I came to a complete halt at the four way stop, at the corner of Pima and Cave Creek Road.

"Yes, I think you're right, Stanford looks better than Wisconsin, and remember they are the team that handed Oregon their only loss of the season. Too bad Oregon lost that game to Stanford because I think Alabama and an Oregon matchup would have been a great BCS Championship game," Kurt chimes in on the football analyzation.

Harold's Corral isn't near as busy as I thought it would be with three or four different college bowl games being played. The areas surrounding the two bars were filled elbow to elbow, however the rest of the bar and restaurant was thirsty and starving for customers. JP D. another fellow student from Thunderbird had joined Kurt and I for a bloody mary and to watch the game. JP was originally from Wisconsin so he had added incentive in cheering for the white and red Badgers and cursing the Cardinal of Stanford. It wasn't a pretty game for either side of the field, although Stanford did walk away victorious with a 20 – 14 win.

Kurt and I exchanged our goodbyes and I told him to have a great time in the Philippines where he was headed for relaxation the latter part of January. He also had a Kenyan safari trip planned with his mother, brother, sister and nephew. Kurt was a true T-Bird, as was I, we both loved to explore and travel the world when given the opportunity.

My phone rang, I looked at the display and saw the name John Smith and answered the ring. John had finished playing his gig at Greasewood Flats and wanted to know if I cared to stop by and have a quick drink with him. "Sure, why not?" had been my reply and I turned onto the dirt road path that leads to the old wood shanty where drinks and food can be ordered. I met a couple of John's friends, Brick and a different Rich, and a few others who had come to watch him perform and then three of us headed over to Pinnacle Peak where he sang a couple of country tunes to the dinner crowd. My amigo, bartender Keith was a little perplexed that John hadn't sang any of Elvis' tunes. To tell the truth, I wish he would have as well. The liquor had flowed strongly in John's direction so I drove him home to Cave Creek, leaving his vehicle at Greasewood Flats overnight.

That is how my year 2012 ended and my year 2013 began, both at Pinnacle Peak; one of the most visited landmark restaurants in Scottsdale and in the greater Phoenix area. When and if you should visit Arizona, have dinner at Pinnacle Peak and pack an old tie in your luggage to wear. Your food server will snip it off and hang it amid the other tens of thousands of ties that entered the building before you and your tie did. No need to dress up, just put the tie on in the parking lot with your unmatched golf shirt, blouse, shorts or jeans. Many celebrities have sat down for a hearty, cowboy style meal including Jerry Lewis. Mr. Lewis was visiting Pinnacle Peak for a famous steak dinner cooked by Marvin "Big Marv" Dickson as was a thieving varmit, that same night. The thief grabbed the partial tie that had been cut by the waitress and made a mad dash for the door while knocking over the glass case that housed three diamondback rattlesnakes. The ruckus caused by the slithering rattlesnakes allowed the culprit to make a clean getaway with a remnant of the tie worn by the famous, comedian actor, Labor Day telethon host and the charitable pal of thousands of children afflicted with muscular dystrophy which he considers them all to be "Jerry's Kids."

Rico & Connie in Palm Springs.

Chapter 16
Snoqualmie Pass

January 6, 2013;

I get up, stretch while taking a shower and wander into the living room where Connie is watching some cop show, it might have been "Law and Order." I'm looking forward to being back in the saddle at work again tomorrow morning, early flight to Portland departing at 6:45 am and then a drive to Seattle to pick up a co-worker to give a presentation for the next day. Laundry needs to be done or else my underwear selection will either be extremely limited or I'll have to go commando for a couple of days. I print out a few things off the computer, send a couple of work related emails and pay bills. I write out checks and pay my bills the old fashioned way. If my money is going to leave me, at least I want the satisfaction of writing and signing the checks; I don't like the idea of my computer just arbitrarily sending off funds electronically into cyber space.

January 7th, 2013; 4:00 am

Alarms going off simultaneously is not the best wake up sound for a Monday morning; however, it is quite effective and arousing. I bounce from my restless sleep into a full, uneasy awakeness, knowing that in umpteen hours I can once again lay my head on a pillow and my body to rest on hopefully a comfortable bed somewhere in Washington near a ski resort.

Shower is super hot, eases the aches in my lower back, knees and .... I've spent too much time in the soothing shower as shown by my Blackberry as I check for any new messages. 4:37 am is not a good time when looking at a 6:45 am flight from PHX to PDX and having only towel dried. Hurriedly, I put on my underwear which includes T-shirt & shorts with a pair of socks. I'd already shaven and brushed my teeth; however, I had yet not driven to the airport nor had I checked my luggage or gone through security.

Southwest Airlines is at Terminal 4. Like a good guy saving a semi–bad guy in a movie, the bus pulled up to the curb and announced that Terminal 4 was being entered onto. I sprang like a female cottontail rabbit about to be mounted by Peter Cottontail with my toolbox, large suitcase that weighed less than 50 pounds and my laptop with copied handouts. These handouts would make the difference between a successful presentation and one with high hopes of becoming a semi- successful presentation.

Dollar was the rental car that gave me an incredible lease / rent of which I might be able to fulfill my work duties! I had arrived at nearly 9:00 am into Portland and needed breakfast in the worst way.

Snoqualmie Pass in Washington state is not a picnic area in the winter, nor is it the absolute, first place in which You might find an ogre or troll. The exit was number 52 off Interstate 90 headed east toward Spokane from Seattle. Mike who is a coworker of mine, of whom I had picked up at the SeaTac airport just an hour before, talked of the meeting we were going to. As we conversed, he and I watched the temperature slowly drop as did the snow. 38 degrees, 37, 35, I slowed from sixty five miles per hour to fifty five, then to forty as the LCD reading of the temperature continued to drop to freezing and beyond. Approximately twelve feet of snow greeted us, along with the yellow loader clearing the parking lot of the Summit Inn. We both put on our winter jackets that were stuffed away in luggage before heading into the building while pulling our suitcases and lugging our laptops. We would check in and then be off to find the Sahalie Ski Lodge where our customers would be staying, bunk and dorm style. The 14,500 square foot lodge with four stories equipped with three fireplaces and a tremendous size dining room was a beautiful sight surrounded by the color of white with fir trees rising towards the heavens.

We had agreed a couple of weeks earlier that most of us attending the sales event would that evening meet at the restaurant / bar at Summit Inn to watch the National BCS (Bowl Championship Series) or as I call it the 'Bullshit Championship Sucks.' Mike & I arrived just as kick off had begun; each of us ordering some dinner and a beverage. By the time the others had arrived at the beginning of the 2nd quarter, Alabama had a sizeable lead over Notre Dame and interest in the game was as lost as were the Fighting Irish of ND. At the start of the fourth quarter, everyone was clearing out so, I headed up to my room as did Mike and a couple of other manufacturer reps to perhaps finish watching the 'Crimson Tide' roll the Catholic University.

The Summit Inn looked quite inviting in the lobby area as there was a real fir Christmas tree wholly (no pun intended) decorated with lights, bulbs, tinsel and with more bulbs and lights and tinsel. There was a trophy size elk head on display above the check in counter with over sized ceilings that reached above the second floor with varnished wood logs neatly embedded together. Once you hauled your luggage up the one flight of stairs, that is when Casper the Friendly Ghost leaves and a not so friendly ghost seems to arrive. The hallway is long, dark and the flooring laid with what seemed to resemble cheap, outdoor carpeting.

My room was only two doors from being at the complete other end, near the red, glowering EXIT sign. Exit was what I indeed wanted to do. Mike's room was near the entrance and the lobby, where I yearned to be. Half jokingly, I whispered loudly, "This looks like the hallway of 'The Shining' with Jack Nicholson."

"Yes, it does," agreed Mike and he added, "if I see a kid on a tricycle riding through the hall, I'll call you."

"Mike, you'd better lock your door tonight, because I have a feeling that I'm going to be both cold and scared tonight," I said, as he put his key into the door lock and I continued my long trek into the manmade tunnel of which I could barely see light at its end.

I turned the heat up high, found the remote and the game, but was having a difficult time hearing the television as the loader was being operated as a snow shovel right outside my back window. I looked out and saw the removal of several feet on snow pushed into a long, wide bank. In the distance I could see the flashing yellow light of a snow plow on the Interstate and an occasional lone trucker pass by. At this instance, the lights flickered and then the TV and all other power of electricity ceased for a few seconds and then the lights came back on to their normal mode; however, the television just had black and white lines running continuously across the screen that eerily resembled many horror movies. I leapt to the phone with only my long underwear over my short underwear and dialed Mike's room number. Thankfully, he answered on the second ring and said, "Yes?"

To this I immediately responded, "Mike, did your power and television set go off?"

"Yeah, the lights flickered a couple of times, but the TV is still down."

"Oh good, I was hoping it wasn't just my room," I nervously chuckled and said, "Goodnight."

I knew that Alabama had won the game, I just didn't know by how much until later the next day.

January 8th, 2013;

The Dodge Journey vehicle was covered with a good eight inches of white powder and a heavy layer of frost iced to the windows below that. I quietly thanked GOD for leading me to Arizona, land of warm, hot and sometimes very hot. After scraping the important windows for driving purposes, Mike and I drove the short distance to the Sahalie Ski Lodge where we had been invited for breakfast the evening prior.

After finding a suitable parking spot off the side of the road since the parking lot was unusable and closed because of the massive snow dump for the last couple of weeks, we hiked uphill to the lodge. We had our hands full with presentation materials, pamphlets and tools which made reaching our destination of over a hundred yards in the icy tundra even more gruesome. I had hiking boots snugly placed around my feet, but Mike had none. He wore his professional black soled dress shoes and lost his footing on the slick roadway before we had reached the incline path that led to the front door of warmth and food. Mike hit the snow packed roadway hard, bounced back up quickly for a man in his thirties even though Mike was much nearer his seventies.

"Are you hurt?" I blurted, as I felt his pain through the scene I had witnessed.

"No, I think I'm alright. Wow, that was quick, wasn't it?"

"Yeah, one second you're walking and the next your feet were in the air and you were on your back. I can't believe how quickly you got back on your feet. You're pretty agile for an old man," I teased.

Just at that moment a voice from the darkness addressed us, "We lost power last night, but we've got a couple of small generators going and a huge fire. Go on up the hill and warm yourselves."

It was then, that we saw the man who resembled a lumberjack equipped with tools, axe and a flashlight that he decided to turn on, to point the way to the lone building in the snow. We thanked him and continued our treacherous climb in hopes of finding food and shelter very quickly as I am from Arizona and Mike is from Southern California. How long we'd survive in temperatures like this were questionable and neither of us wanted to explore our bodily limits.

Upon reaching the summit or entrance to the front door we both stomped our feet to remove all clinging snow and ice from our shoes. The building was dark, however, after we entered the hallway that led to the stairs we could see flickering lights either from a candle or a flashlight. Turned out to be both, some of the persons had candles while a couple others had flashlights.

"Hello, welcome; we'll have breakfast ready in a few minutes, go on upstairs to the kitchen and dining room. Some of the guys are cooking eggs and bacon on the grill outside. Maintenance is working on getting power back to us. Try and make yourselves at home," greeted the female half of the caretaking couple that were assigned to watch over the lodge, during the month of January.

The Sahalie Ski Lodge is jointly owned by its members and some of them volunteer to care for the lodge and help with accommodations for visitors and special events such as this. There is a very interesting story about this place on the Internet if you care to learn more. The original lodge was burned to the ground as a result of an accident; but, no casualties and the lodge was rebuilt.

Sure enough, three brave souls were around the enormous grill just outside the front door on the patio while a group of us watched intently on the inside, through the gigantic plate glass windows at our eggs being scrambled to perfection by the heroic fast order cooks with candles in hand on the outside braving the freezing temperatures. The breakfast was epic, when I've tasted better eggs and bacon, I know not.

Eventually, when the sun finally raised, the natural sunlight streaming through the windows allowed for the sales event to begin. The power was restored around 10:30 am and all's well that ends well. The next morning,

I dropped Mike off at the car rental facility near the SeaTac International Airport and pointed my car in the southern direction on Interstate 5 back to Portland.

A day later and I was back in sunny Arizona.

Sahalie Ski Club & Lodge at Snoqualmie Pass in the state of Washington.

Chapter 17
The Rest of the Story?

January 11th, 2013;

My amigo John P. (yes another John in the story) calls me up, his wife and daughter are out of town and he wants to go have a drink. He comes by the house and picks me up, we head over to 'The Hideaway' for a quick Corona and then over to 'Harold's' for a margarita while listening to a country band. John P. and I discuss the issue and my worries of the needle incident. He tells me that I'm too damn mean to die just yet and I have to agree.

January 14th, 2013;

Late afternoon I drive to Casa Grande and check into the Holiday Inn so as to be ready for a tire repair seminar that I'll be giving early the next morning in Eloy, Arizona and then visiting with customers in the area for the following days left in the week.

January 18th, 2013;

I drive over to Buddy Stubbs Harley Davidson to drop off a copy of the epic, adventure, "My Bad Tequila," as Buddy Stubbs was mentioned in the book. I gave it to one of the his salesman who tells me that Buddy still comes in to give the guided tour of his motorcycle museum every Saturday at noon.

Later that afternoon, John Dennis Smith calls and asks Connie and I to come over for a pig roast. One of his buddies drew a javelina tag and killed a wild pig which was being barbequed over a hot, brick pit at his and Lisa's home. We drive over to sample the pig and it is not bad which means it was not good. After enjoying the fire with them and some of their neighbors, I tell John that I need to talk with him, so the both of us wandered around to the back side of the property.

"John, as you know I am almost done writing my book and then I'll be getting back to your story and I have a question for you" I stated.

He then said, "Sure, what is it?"

"I'd like to get your permission to use the picture of you and Elvis in my book, can I get the original?"

"Not a problem, amigo; but, I don't have it here with me."

"Thanks, I think it will be a great addition to the book," I added and we walked back to the fire.

Later that evening, "we all decided to go into Harold's for some good ribs and chicken wings since the roasted javelina hadn't filled our appetites. One of my favorite Arizona bands, Mogollon is playing and Sarah Palin is there with her husband, Todd, enjoying dinner and drinks with some of their friends from Arizona. I walk out to my Xterra and grab a copy of 'My Bad Tequila,' sign it and personalize it with: "Amiga Sarah, Enjoy the Mystery & Adventure of 'My Bad Tequila'" and take it to her table. She's at the far end, so I just ask her friends to pass it on down to her, I wave at her and walk back to the bar to join my wife and the others.

January 24th, 2013;

"Hello Rico, how are you doing?" greeted Dr. Robert Rauscher as he entered one of the waiting rooms where I had been seated just minutes before, with Stephanie checking my vitals of heart rate, temperature, weight and blood pressure.

"Feeling great, Dr. Rauscher and you?" I pleasantly responded.

"This is a medical student that I have here with me, do you mind if he sits in on our conversation?" the Doctor asked.

"Sure, that will be fine, I'm here to see you about another blood test," I explained.

"Yes, that is right, it has now been three months hasn't it," he then added, "go ahead and please have a seat up here," he pointed to the retractable half bed with the fresh sheet of paper covering it. "I'll have you go in for five different blood tests including HIV and syphilis. If your tests come up negative then you should be about 75% clear of contracting the virus. After six months testing with negative results the odds are real favorable, about 90% that you're fine. I don't remember if we talked about this last time; but, I believe the chances of you having contracted the HIV virus very low as the virus can not live very long in the open air. Also, there are some people who are immune to HIV and AIDS as there have been cases of homosexual men having unprotected anal intercourse with other homosexual men for years and they have never contracted the virus or disease. Is everything else alright with you?" he finished.

"Thank you for explaining that to me, I do feel much better about this," I assured myself and the doctor.

The three of us somehow got into an interesting discussion of ethics between teachers and their students, between doctors and their patients. I then received my paperwork and made the short walk over to the Sonoran Quest Laboratories where a pleasant lady with an English accent called me into a room to take my blood into five clear tubes.

Not wanting the lady to think I was involved in homosexual activities, I volunteered what had happened three months ago while visiting San Francisco. "That is the worst thing I've heard today," Annette said sympathetically.

"Oh, don't worry, I believe I am going to be alright. Got to be positive right, thinking that is," I corrected myself.

Texts sent from John Smith to Rico Austin and vice versa:

February 2nd, 2013; 8:25 pm "Hey u guys want to come to Super bowel (sic) party johnnys mountain at 3pm comebon (sic) bring a dip and a chip all else is provided. Oh Tequilla (sic) to (sic) bring some. lol ok" JS

February 2nd, 2013; 8:30 pm "Can u guys come?" JS

February 2nd, 2013; 8:30 pm: "Yes, sounds good, I just cooked a ham, I'll bring some & tequila!" RA

February 2nd, 2013; 8:30 pm: "Perfect ok bring Connie to (sic) ok lol….JS

February 2nd, 2013; 8:32 pm: "Therre (sic) will be me lisa .. Tim Red And Bruce and Shavon thats all…Coll (sic?) luv u see u then JS

February 3rd, 2013; 4:15 pm: "Where u guys at" JS

We had just pulled in when John's text came through, asking us where we were. Connie and I had missed the singing of the Star Spangled Banner and entered just as the referee was tossing the coin into the air for the San Francisco Forty Niners and the Baltimore Ravens to choose whether or not to receive or kick and which end of the field to defend first.

I was more interested in seeing the commercials than the game. My amigo and former BSU room mate Steve Boyce had told me about the Hyundai commercial in which he is wearing a 45 pound fat suit that makes his 280 pound figure look to be 400 pounds with his fake butt crack showing as he rode a crotch rocket. Hyundai had sent him the clip a few days earlier of which he shared on Facebook. I was able to see the commercial before hand, so I knew exactly what to look for during the game. Boyce had told me to look for him in the 1st quarter, but the ad showed in the 2nd quarter and the butt crack scene had been cut. He was able to show his genuine acting skills with a blown kiss to the driver and his wife in their 2013 Hyundai Sonata Turbo as they pass him and other obstacles on the highway. It was pretty exciting to see Steve in his first Super Bowl commercial even though I had seen him in several other commercials, television series and playing character roles as an extra in a couple of movies.

Another Hollywood friend, Don Yates who has the nickname of "Hollywood" Yates was also to be in his first Super Bowl ad; however, all of his shots in the Lincoln car commercial had been cut, so a bit of disappointment for him, his friends and family. Just so happened that both Steve and Don were watching the Super Bowl together with other musicians and actors in Capistrano Beach at the Surfin' Cowboy. I didn't even know that they knew each other since my relationship with each of them is separate and of its own. I found out on Facebook when Steve sent me an invite a week earlier to join them all on the Southern California coast, if at all possible. It is indeed, a 'Small World!'

At half time John and I did a shot of Azunia Tequila and I again asked him about the picture of him when he was a toddler and being held by his daddy, Elvis. I mentioned to John that I was getting close to finishing my memoirs book and needed to get the picture asap. I added that I would be able to put my efforts toward his book most likely by the end of this month or the beginning of March. "I'll get it to you in a couple of days," he promised.

February 3rd, 2013; 9:30 pm "Luv u guys it was great having u guys over…" JS

February 3rd, 2013; 9:51 pm "Hey where is the place overseas, that the Col. Didntt (sic) let Elvis play you told me about before ? And do u know someone there we can speak with to possible (sic) book a show there? JS

February 4th, 2013; 11:38 am "Staffard (sic) England, also if you want I'll try to book you singin' one afternoon in Mexico" RA

February 4th , 2013; 11:38 am "Ok yea cool that would be so cool u mean when we go down you know a place.." JS

February 4th, 2013; 11:40 am "And i want to talk to you about the book I want u to write about me.. And the story about the song World we Will Be Late Today,. JS

February 13th, 2013;
An email from AuthorHouse stating that my Children's book, "ARIZONA Is Where I Live," is ready for me to approve on their website. I type in the name of the book and the cover photo comes up with the blurb of 'about the illustrator' instead of 'about the book" with several typos and the 'preview of the book' is from the first initial text, not the finished product.

I send back an email and copied each person at AuthorHouse of which Connie and I have dealt with from the very beginning. There have been mistake after mistake and a language barrier as we were assigned a team from the Philippines and not an American team from Indiana. I called my salesperson and told him the only way I would continue on with my other book projects, is if I had a guarantee that my next teams, would be their absolute best from stateside in Indiana. An agreement was settled and I await for the first project to be finished so that I may work on getting this memoir and autobiography to them. I hope for much fewer mistakes as my confidence in this publisher is as low as my confidence is with Wells Fargo bank in their land loan department (separate issue, but the same type of incompetence and lack of ownership or responsibility).

February 18th, 2013; President's Day

It's a Monday morning and I have the day off to celebrate President's Day of which I use the entire day to write. Connie calls me mid day to see how I'm doing. "Looks as if I'll go over the 50,000 word threshold today and possibly finish writing "In the Shadow of Elvis, Perils of a Ghostwriter," I shared with her.

"Do you still want to go to the movies this afternoon to see 'The Impossible?'" she asks.

"If you don't mind, can we go later this week? I'm in a great writing mood, finished editing and just cruising on the book today."

"Sure, maybe we'll try and go Wednesday or Thursday evening."

"Great, let's go on a walk as soon as you get home then. I'll be ready for a break, away from the computer and writing."

Chapter 18
The Sting!

February 18th, 2013; Early afternoon

Life is grand, I've surpassed 51,000 words on my memoirs novel. According to many critics 50,000 words must be written for your writing to be considered a novel.

I feel that sometime this evening I will pen, "The End."

Texts from John Dennis Smith to Rico Austin and vice versa:

February 18th, 2013; 3:22 pm "Hey my buddy Skippy want a signd (sic) book Of your book" JS

February 18th, 2013; 3:23 pm "No Problema" RA

February 18th, 2013; 3:24 pm "Where u at" JS

February 18th, 2013; 3:25 pm "Home sweet home" RA

February 18th, 2013; 3:27 pm "We have to get together soon I am ready for you to get the World be late today book" JS

February 18th, 2013; 3:27 pm "Ok my other book is coming oit (sic) its done and almost on line" JS

I do a double take on the text, "What the heck is John texting about,"

I think to myself. "I'm writing his book, we shook hands on it and John told me that from where he is from, a handshake is a man's word."

We had talked of the song, "World We Will Be Late Today," but, my idea had been to include the download with the book. I loved hearing John sing that song and had told him so. Each time I listened to it, I did indeed hear his Daddy's voice come from through the vocal cords of his son, John.

February 18th, 2013; 3:28 pm "Amigo what's the other book?" RA

February 18th, 2013; 3:33 pm "Let the boy sing book !!!" JS

February 18th, 2013; 3:36 pm "I thought I was doing that, what happened?" RA

February 18th, 2013; 3:36 pm "Your (sic) doing the other book with the song world will be late today the sequel book" JS

February 18th, 2013; 3:39 pm "The frist (sic) book is out of my hands but world be late book is me and you If u still will writevit (sic)" JS

February 18th, 2013; 3:40 pm "Write it" JS

February 18th, 2013; 3:40 pm "Who wrote the other one?" RA

February 18th, 2013; 3:44 pm "Just me as author and Rich as collaberator (sic) the publisher Tate ... Published it…Its out on the 20th of march… JS

February 18th, 2013; 3:45 pm "Theres (sic) a site Let the Boy Sing Face book page go there and see it and hit like" JS

February 18th, 2013; 3:46 pm "I didn't get to choose" JS

February 18th, 2013; 3:48 pm "I can't find the page" RA

February 18th, 2013; 3:54 pm "Go to john d smith presley personal page then right under the picture of me sitting with guitar touch let the boy sing" JS

February 18th, 2013; 3:59 pm "Did u find it" JS

February 18th, 2013; 4:05 pm "Yes, I'm just sick, I thought I was doing it" RA

February 18th, 2013; 4:05 pm "Happy for you but not for Rich" RA

February 18th, 2013; 4:14 pm "I know but I did save great stuff for mine and your book if you will write it with me World will be Late Today book like we talked about.." JS

February 18th, 2013; 4:15 pm "Did you see the site" JS

February 18th, 2013; 4:16 pm "I want to start advertising the Sequel book when your (sic) ready to on the sites to.. About the time you have it written it will be time to get it out" JS

I can't even bring myself to send another text back. I'm devastated by the amount of time, work and effort I had spent with John, taking notes, chatting about his past and spending hours upon hours thinking about how John must have felt as a boy, as a young man and now as a middle aged man. I was about to finish the book, I was writing the final conclusion, Chapter 17 and now a surprise ending for the author and the reader. I found out about the unhappy ending just minutes before writing and adding this 18th Chapter.

Handshakes must mean nothing, the old West has been beaten by the new Wave. I guess Rich Carl…. got the last laugh and was correct in telling me on that November day that he was in charge and told me to write whatever I wanted, because I would not be writing 'Let the Boy Sing,' It does hurt to type those four words on my screen.

Shame on me for trusting on a handshake and friendship. I should have known better, once again I had set myself up for disappointment with

John Dennis Smith. I know that he is a good guy that just got sucked into listening and following the wicked direction of Rich Carl...., as I could tell from our meetings that this fellow had a noose around John's neck and he just keeps pulling it a little tighter as time drifts by.

After all that has happened these last seven or eight months, I must consider one thing: I do have more in common with homosexual men or others that may have been in contact with HIV and or AIDS than I ever thought possible. Our worries are exactly the same when we enter through those glass doors into the blood center to have our blood checked and evaluated; wondering, pondering if our blood is still clean, uncontaminated and untarnished of an awful, deadly virus. Most of us in this or some other precarious situation look at each special instance and day with an unblemished sight, hopeful that we may once again experience many more beautiful days and pleasures, whether great or of the smallest magnitude, with our cherished, loved ones.

I'm not condoning unsafe or protected homosexual intercourse and I am not bashing it either. It is not my way of life, just as others, most likely find fault with the way I choose to live. The thing that I truly know is that we are all one species; no matter what race, religion, color, sexual preference, age, gender or national origin. We are all of the human race and need to show kindness toward one another. I am not gay, but I do understand the plight they face a bit more than I did before.

I sat by the front window and stared out into the desert watching a lone coyote trot worriless into the horizon at sunset, while I waited for a white SUV to drive up the dirt road and pull into the garage. I needed to tell Connie that I loved her, appreciated her and that a minor change in plans had taken place; but, I would wait to tell her, face to face, not on the phone. She too, had put a great deal of energy into the project, working with several different ideas on the cover, staying up late and spending her few, free, precious weekends perfecting our vision of what we anticipated would sell and interest the masses. I do think that I took the news better than did she, as she just kept saying, "How could John do this to you? He knew you had spent hours and hours on him and his book. He promised!"

"Let's go for a walk and talk about this, okay," I warmly suggested.

We both put on our tennis shoes and headed down the familiar, dirt path. I felt the pain in my stomach, the anger in my head and the hurt in my heart; but, chose to try and take the high, paved road. "It's spilt milk now, nothing we can do except look on the bright side. I'm a much better writer and story teller than either Rich or John. My book has the meat and potatoes of the Elvis story plus everything else that has happened of which I have written, and John has been kind enough to give me full carte blanche of all his personal photos to use in the book.

The main thing is, hopefully, I don't have HIV or AIDS. Everything else doesn't matter. I have you Babe!"

Connie smiled slightly and said, "I do feel, so bad for you."

"Please don't be upset, it will all workout, I've already built up quite a readership of people that loved, 'My Bad Tequila' and those same readers of great taste will want to read my next bestselling book, 'In the Shadow of Elvis, Perils of a Ghostwriter,'" and managed to show a positive spirit in my eyes.

As I finish my walk, unlatch the gate to the backyard, see my reflection in the swimming pool and enter through the backdoor into our home; I wander over to the laptop, look all the papers of research strewn across the dining room table and it was then that I recognized a familiar pang, this time in the heart. I felt as if I had been stung once again, by the desert's scorpion.

Hopefully, not, THE END!

"Maybe tomorrow will be better!"

Rico Austin – Mi Vida Loca
(Biography)

Born and raised in Southwestern Idaho, Rico is the oldest of five boys, growing up in an area that was ripe for several adventures for him, his four younger brothers and numerous cousins.

Rico grew up near farmland that produced potatoes, hay, hops, grain and corn. There were several fruit orchards and vineyards in the Snake River Valley as well, due to the extraordinary fertile soil. A few years out of high school he moved to (the big city) of Boise and enrolled at Boise State University as a student and walk- on football player. However, he could not escape the allure of traveling the world and began writing and storing his experiences in hopes of someday becoming a novelist. He began by reading every chance he had. From contemporary novels to classical literature, Rico's love of storytelling was uncontrollable. He appeared occasionally at Boise's former Comedy Club as a "Stand Up Comedian," retelling his stories of growing up in a comedic fashion.

Rico earned an Associate Degree in Marketing and Sales from BSU. After a few years of low level management positions, Rico moved to Hawaii for a short time surfing the waters of Kauai and enjoying the outdoors. He then moved to Southern California for less than a year before heading back to Idaho. In 1991, Rico moved to the Phoenix/Scottsdale area and continued his education receiving a Bachelors of Business Administration in International Business at Grand Canyon University and received "Outstanding International Business Graduate of 1995." That same year he was also selected as "Mr. Future Business Executive" at the State Leadership Conference which included all universities in the State of Arizona.

The summer before graduating Rico went to Vilnius, Lithuania and taught English (ESL). During fall semester of his senior year at GCU, Rico attended Staffordshire University in England where he also started on the American Football Team for the Staffordshire Stallions. Rico finished his Masters, an MBA in International Management at Thunderbird School of Global Management with a focus on the Latin American Region and the Spanish language. He did this while working full time as a feature writer and free lance journalist at the T-Bird school paper, "DAS TOR." A few of his articles at "DAS TOR" were written in Spanish by Rico, specially for the foreign students of Latin America.

Former Vice President Dan Quayle served as an "Invited Interim Professor" by the Thunderbird School President, Dr. Roy Herberger for 2 semesters and Rico was fortunate enough to be one of 16 students selected to attend his class. *Special note, Rico received an "A" from the VP for the 2 credit elective class. Was it because of Rico's performance on studies or VP Quayle was afraid of what Mr. Austin might write in the paper?

Hollywood has even had an encounter with Rico. For those of you who watched Baywatch with the beautiful Pamela Anderson and David Hasselhoff, Mr. Rico Austin did a cameo appearance in the episode, "Night of the Dolphin" in 1997, where he played the role of a drug lord on a huge yacht with sexy chicks. He and his graduate class mates watched the aired episode in the "old clock tower hanger," together in the TV lounge. He was invited back for another episode by Casting Director Susie Glickman, but had to decline due to a conflict with finals at Thunderbird. Rico chose education over stardom, when questioned why, he responded, "No one can ever take your education away. Everything else can come and go and, most likely will." Rico also acted in a commercial for the local market in Boise, ID as a construction worker in "That old House," sponsored by BMC West.

Rico is an avid fisherman and has traveled far and wide to cast his line into many waters; including streams, lakes, ponds, rivers, seas and oceans.

He has worked for a few international companies as both a sales manager and a marketing manager. In his spare time he has worked as a Land Developer and was a Licensed Realtor in Arizona. Should you decide to visit Arizona, Rico would be more than happy to show you around his

Great State of Arizona through his Children's book, "ARIZONA Is Where I Live."

Rico is happily married to a graphic artist from Minnesota with a prominent company. They make their homes in the "Land of the Sun," Scottsdale, Arizona and San Carlos, Sonora, Mexico. He and his wife Connie enjoy snorkeling, hiking, hanging by their swimming pool and traveling to the different beaches of Mexico while sipping on a cold cerveza or margarita blended with Rico's favorite TEQUILA.

Rico Austin first began writing seriously as a seventh grader at age 13. He was elected as reporter for the "Eager Beaver 4-H Club" in Marsing, Idaho and started submitting weekly articles to the local newspaper. Rico then was elected reporter for the local FFA chapter his freshman and sophomore year, continuing to expand his writing ability. As a freshman Rico took 3rd place in the Marsing High School essay contest titled "American Beef Farmers."

He later would later become a professional freelance and feature writer for DAS TOR newspaper at Thunderbird Global School of Management from 1996 – 1998. Rico also won the first and only writing essay at DAS TOR in March 1997. The essay asked contestants to propose ways for Thunderbird to be improved. Rico used his humor, knowledge of several countries that he had visited and innovation to secure the winning essay.

One of his most serious assignments and pieces of journalism was reporting on the Winterim class 97, "US Foreign Economic Policy" in Washington DC including the opening of the 105th Congress and the Inauguration of the President of the United States - Mr. Bill Clinton.

Rico was selected for the May 19th, 2013 issue to represent Arizona in fellow author, Annette Synder's popular blog, "Fifty Authors from Fifty States," which spotlights writing professionals across the Fifty United States. http://annettesnyder.blogspot.com

Rico was also chosen from among several hundred writers and bloggers to help compile a booklet with 13 other prominent authors. "How to Create Credibility as a Freelancer - 70 Tips from a Collection of Experts" was published in 12/2009. To purchase the Booklet: leave a message in Guest Book at: http://site.mybadtequila.com/Guestbook

Website: www.RicoAustin.com

Favorite movie, "Gone With the Wind"
Favorite comedy, "Hangover"

His favorite books are:
John Steinbeck's "East of Eden"
Ernest Hemingway's "The Old Man and the Sea"
J.R. Tolkien's "The Hobbit"
David Stuart's "The Guaymas Chronicles"
Jack London's "Call of the Wild"
E.B. White's "Charlotte's Web"
Wilson Rawls' "Where the Red Fern Grows"

Rico's first novel, "MY BAD TEQUILA" was published in September of 2010. His first Children's book, "ARIZONA Is Where I Live" was published February 14th of 2013. This is the same day as Arizona's 101st Birthday.

The Hit Single Song, "My Bad Tequila" co-written by Rico and Elly Garrison, who also sings and performs the song with her band QuarterDeck, can be found on iTunes, Yahoo Music and Amazon Music. www.QuarterDeckCountry.com

H. Joseph Erhmann, Rico Austin & Julio Bermejo
at Tommy's Mexican Restaurant in San Francisco, CA;
also pictured, Azunia Tequila!

Rico & Connie in San Carlos, Sonora, Mexico
also pictured: Tetakawi Mountain & Sea of Cortez.

Feliz Hanukkah, Feliz Navidad & Feliz Ano Nuevo - Amigas & Amigos

The Award winning novel, "My Bad Tequila"
www.Amazon.com & BarnesAndNoble.com

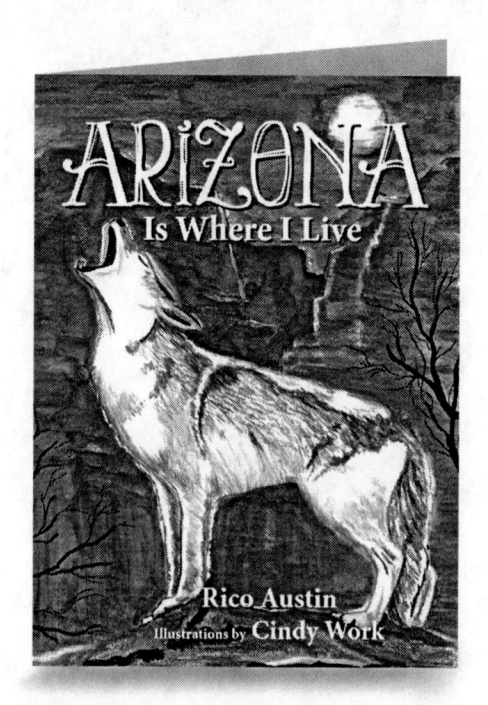

The new children's book, "ARIZONA Is Where I Live"
www.AuthorHouse.com
www.Amazon.com & www.BarnesAndNoble.com

Check out "My Bad Tequila" Blog at:
http://blog.mybadtequila.com

Follow us on Twitter
@mybadtequila and @ricoaustin

"Like" us on Facebook at:
"In the Shadow of ELVIS, Perils of a Ghostwriter"

&

"Official My Bad Tequila Fan Page"